History of Harlow

History of Harlow

Edited by Linley H. Bateman

Harlow Development Corporation

Printed in England at the Shenval Press, London, Hertford and Harlow

Foreword

This book is not the first record of the history of Harlow. Canon John L. Fisher, in his concern to chronicle many features of a past manner of life which would tend to be obliterated by the construction of the new town, wrote his book *Harlow New Town—A Short History of the Area which it will embrace* published in January 1951 and now long out of print. In his book he paid tribute to earlier historians—Morant and Newcourt, to the rich records preserved by the great monasteries of Bury St Edmunds and Waltham Holy Cross, and to the information available from parochial records, Quarter Sessions rolls, estate surveys and tithe maps.

Since the publication of Canon Fisher's book the face of Harlow has changed dramatically. The centuries-old village and manorial pattern, while not lost, is now obscured. At the same time more information about the past has come to light, and it seems appropriate that 1968—the twenty-first anniversary of the new town of Harlow—should be commemorated by the preparation of a new *History of Harlow*.

Fortunately, the changes in Harlow during the past twenty-one years do not mean that all physical vestiges of the past have been lost. Many of the buildings constructed by our predecessors still exist and can be seen. Much of the road pattern—some of it very ancient in origin—still exists, often in the form of cycle tracks. Most of the old villages, the old inns and churches, remain in our town. It is hoped that this book will help in their rediscovery by many who were perhaps hardly aware of their existence.

John Newsom
Chairman
Harlow Development Corporation

The Museum Workshop, which is the first step towards establishing a Harlow Museum, is situated in the Town Park adjacent to Spurriers and contains many documents and objects of historical interest related to Harlow and to the surrounding area. It provides a base for both the amateur and the professional working in this field.

At the time of going to print in January 1969, the Museum Workshop is open on Thursday evenings from 5.30 pm, on Saturdays from 10.0 am to 5.0 pm and on Wednesday and Friday evenings by arrangement. (Telephone 21668.)

Acknowledgements

Those who have contributed to this book will agree that the first acknowledgement must go to Canon John L. Fisher who dedicated so much time and energy to the initial assembly, from many different sources, of the material used in his book *Harlow New Town—A Short History of the Area which it will embrace* published in January 1951. It has proved possible to use much of Canon Fisher's work in this new *History of Harlow*.

However, since Canon Fisher's book was written, new information has come to light, and has been incorporated herein. In particular we are indebted to:

Mr A. V. B. Gibson, Dip Arch Lond, for Chapter 1 dealing with pre-Roman history, who in turn has been assisted by the Harlow Historical and Archaeological Society, Mr C. Partridge of the East Herts and St Albans' Archaeological Societies, Mr J. Moss-Eccardt, MA, of Letchworth Museum, and Major K. E. Wilson, BSc(Eng), AMIEE, of Sawbridgeworth.

Dr N. E. France, BSc, MB, BCh, FCPath, assisted by Miss B. M. Gobel and Mr B. J. Steel, all of the West Essex Archaeological Group, for Chapter 2 dealing with Roman Harlow.

Mr S. W. Chance for material used in Chapters 3–12. With the exception of Chapters 10 and 11, these draw substantially on Canon Fisher's material, but with revisions and additions based on more up-to-date information. For Chapters 10 and 11 Mr Chance has contributed material gleaned from various sources, as indicated in the bibliography at the back of the book.

For Chapter 13—Harlow since 1947—I, as Editor, must take the main responsibility. It draws extensively on official archives and, in particular, the Corporation's own records. It could not have been compiled without the help which has been given by the staff of the Corporation and for the later years by the staff of the Urban District Council. We are all perhaps too close to the events set out in this chapter, and too involved in the life of the town to make final and objective judgements about what has been achieved. All we can do is to set out the key facts and await the verdict of history.

We are also indebted to Mr Christopher Newsom and Mr J. S. W. Gibson of Messrs Longmans Green & Co Ltd, for technical advice, and also for reading the complete text and making valuable comments on it. The text was similarly submitted to Mr L. A. Ward, ALA, the

Librarian of the Town Centre Library where much information of historical significance for the town is available. The help of Mr Ward and his staff was of the greatest value.

Both Mr Chance and myself would wish to pay tribute to help received from the Essex Record Office, where so much information about Harlow is available, and to Mr S. Eglinton-Mead, Harlow's Museum's Officer, especially in connection with the genealogy of some of the families referred to in this book.

Thanks are also given to members of staff of the Development Corporation's Architect Department who drew the map at the end of the book, using historical material provided by our contributors. They also drew the diagrams illustrating aspects of the Master Plan for the town, and, under the guidance of Dr France, drew the 'impression' of the Roman Temple.

We are indebted to the following for permission to reproduce certain photographs and maps in this book:

Essex Record Office—Altham map, page 54.

Harlow Central Library—Chapman and André map, pages 88, 89.

      —Photograph of Cock Inn, facing page 97.

Fox Photos Ltd—photographs of Royal Visit, facing page 128.

Linley H. Bateman
Editor

Contents

List of illustrations

Introduction
The origin of the name of Harlow

A Saxon tribe settled in this district and called it Harlow. The name was applied first to the whole tribal area, and then to the principal settlement within it. This name is composed of two Saxon words—'here', meaning an army or host, and 'hlaw' meaning a hill. An artificial mound standing on fairly high ground above the centre of the district no doubt served as the assembly station of the tribal force and afterwards became the meeting-place for the district. This hillock gave Harlow its name; though diminished in height through centuries of wear and overgrown with trees, it is still visible just to the south of Gilden Way. In medieval days the mound was called the 'moot-bury' or hill of meeting; this in course of time became corrupted to 'Mulberry', so both Harlow and Mulberry Green have acquired their names from the same hill.

Though the spelling of Harlow has varied from time to time the pronunciation has remained fairly constant, for the first component 'here' seems to have been pronounced 'hare' or 'har' just as we pronounce Hertford. We get the same 'a' sound in Hare Street or 'army street' which is also derived from the Saxon 'here'. How the Saxons spelt the name is uncertain for the one Saxon document mentioning Harlow—the will of Thurstan—is only preserved in a fourteenth-century transcript. The earliest original source containing the name is Domesday Book; there the name occurs several times, always as Herlaua. It is unlikely that the town was ever called this; the Norman scribes frequently Latinized Saxon names, and as all towns are feminine in Latin they gave to Harlow the customary feminine ending of 'a'. In Norman deeds the name is spelt Herlaue, for the French have no 'w' in normal usage, and 'au' is sounded 'o'. Herlaue continued to be the regular form until the middle of the thirteenth century, when the 'w' reappears, and for the next century and a half the name almost invariably appears as Herlawe. The only exceptions noted are Herlaghe and Herlowe in two transferences of property, one in 1303 and the other in 1305, while in 1323 in an inquest on lands after the death of the holder the name is spelt Harlouwe. In the fifteenth century the spelling grows more fanciful. About the year 1410 we find Harlough, Harlawe, Harlaughe and a little later Harloughe; but by 1430 Harlowe had become the usual spelling and is the commonest form all through the seventeenth century, until the final '———e' was dropped in the time of the Georges. Even so, occasional variants occur. A Parndon court roll of the year 1534 mentions 'the tenant of the chantry of Harloo' and an inscription in St Mary and St Hugh's church, Old Harlow gives the spelling Harloe.

So much for the spelling variations, rather a surprising number for such a simple name. It is, however, only by chance that the town has retained this simple form; it might easily have become a compound name, such as Epping Upland, Bishop's Stortford, Market Rasen and the like. At quite an early date in the thirteenth century when a levy was being made for the Abbot of St Edmunds, the sum was raised in two portions, one from the market and the other from the upland. The name might well have become established as it has in Epping, and we might have had, as there, two separate parishes, Harlow Market and Harlow Upland. This division did actually take place in Victorian times, but the two parishes were only distinguished by the name of the churches and the township remained a single unit. Nevertheless, in the fourteenth century, when the market at Harlow was fairly flourishing, the town was sometimes called Market Harlow, or Chipping Harlow; the register of Bishop Sudbury for the year 1367 records the institution of William de Watlynton to the rectory of Chepyngherlawe. The name did not last, but the area where the first stage of development of the 'new' town took place is still called Chippingfield meaning Market Field.

The Abbot of St Edmunds had another Essex manor at Stapleford, where the Abbot owned half the village and the de Tany family the other; from the twelfth century Stapleford has been split into two villages, Stapleford Abbots and Stapleford Tawney. Harlow, in the same way, was occasionally known as Harlow Abbots, but as there was only one Harlow the distinctive name was pointless and never came into general use. In a conveyance of land in the year 1388 Harlow appears as Great Harlawe, but this seems to be a solitary instance.

Chapter 1
Pre-Roman History

The appearance of the locality in which the modern town of Harlow is situated is utterly different from its appearance at the time our story begins, nearly half a million years ago. However, had the new town not been built, little would have been known of the interesting geology of the region, responsible for its present surface aspect.

Prior to the building of the new town, some 2,000 boreholes were sunk to determine the nature of the subsoil. These revealed a series of laminated clays and sands showing that on three occasions great ice sheets had traversed the area leaving their refuse of stone and silt in thick layers of 'boulder clay'.

These events occurred in the Great Ice Age, a succession of four cold periods with warm periods in between called 'glacials' and 'interglacials' respectively. In addition to ice deposits, there is evidence beneath the town of a mile-wide platform cut into the underlying London Clay. This appears to be the ancient channel of the River Thames when it flowed, not in its present course through London, but following a more northerly route through mid Essex.

Remote geological times are difficult to date in absolute years, but this early channel of the Thames was probably formed about 450,000 years ago. It is of interest to note that an even earlier stage has been traced when the Thames flowed through Hatfield and Bishop's Stortford. Thereafter it has been pushed progressively southwards by successive ice advances. It is probable that the large river estuaries on the east coast of Essex were cut by these ancient channels of the Thames.

The oldest ice advance that can be detected in the vicinity of Harlow has left a sheet of boulder clay perched high on the ridge south of the town at Rye Hill and Epping Long Green. Geologists equate this with the second, i.e. 'Mindel' glaciation and date it at about 476,000 years ago.

Closely following this period the climate became warmer and the Thames cut its channel at the site of the town. The sands filling this channel lie some 60 feet below the Town Centre and we can visualize elephants, sabre-toothed tigers and rhinoceros roaming along the river banks in search of food and water. This channel represents a short warm phase within the Mindel glaciation.

It may be that man had penetrated into Britain by this time, though the evidence is disputable.

This warm period gave way to another cold phase before the climate settled to a very long, warm ('Interglacial') period known as the Great

Interglacial, which began about 400,000 years ago and lasted for about 150,000 years. It is from this period that we find the earliest undisputed remains of man in Britain. The Thames by this time had moved to its present valley, and ancient gravels of the Thames along its present course have yielded a vast number of flint implements of this remote period. The River Stort had apparently been formed at this time, and Fig. 1 shows just such an implement that has been found in the Stort gravels at Sawbridgeworth. This hand axe, as it is called, would have been used for cutting, digging and hammering. To the archaeologist the hand axe is of Acheulian type. Similar hand axes have been found in considerable numbers from sites along the Lea valley.

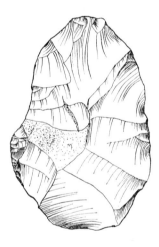

Fig. 1. Acheulian hand axe—
Sawbridgeworth
(Half actual size)

The Great Interglacial closed with the onset of a severe cold period known as the Riss Glaciation, about 230,000 years ago, and great quantities of boulder clay and sand were discharged over the land surface of Essex. At Harlow, two boulder clay spreads, each about 14 feet thick, with an interleaved sand layer 27 feet thick lie directly below the Town Centre as a witness to this glaciation. A fine section of these deposits existed at the Pole Hole pit (see map) and boulder clay overlain by sand can still be seen although it is rather overgrown.

The high ridge at Rye Hill and Epping Long Green acted as a stop to this boulder clay spread and from a good viewing point such as Thornwood or Nazeing, the structure of the landscape is easy to see. To the south, boulder clay of the Mindel glaciation caps the highest ground. To the north the whole area upon which Harlow now stands was excavated by the Thames to a depth of 60 feet to be subsequently back-filled to its present level by the Riss Glaciation deposits.

Between the Thames valley stage and the Riss Glaciation man had visited the region in the Great Interglacial, leaving behind him (for example) the hand axe from Sawbridgeworth which had become incorporated in the gravel of the early Stort.

The glacial period in Britain came to an end about 10,000 B.C. and with the gradual increase in temperature forests spread over temperate Europe. This post-glacial period witnessed the arrival of Mesolithic hunting bands using small refined weapons to hunt and fish. Mesolithic flint tools have been found at High Beech, Waltham Abbey, Broxbourne and Bishop's Stortford, the last three being riverside sites typical of a group of Mesolithic folk whose economy was adapted to forests and rivers. These so-called 'Maglemosian' people used the earliest wood-cutting axes in Europe, made of flint with very sharp edges that were resharpened by trimming. These 'tranchet' axes have been found at each of the Lea-Stort valley sites.

From Harlow a small number of Mesolithic flints have been found at an occupation site at Great Parndon. Here, prehistoric material covering a great range of time has been found eroding out of the side of a disused gravel pit. The site lies at the confluence of the Todd Brook with Canons Brook, on gently sloping ground facing south and it must have been a favoured spot in prehistoric times.

It is of interest also that a pocket of 'loess', a fine wind-blown dust, has been found on the site. If this deposit was more extensive in those days it would have developed a light soil, most favourable to the economy of early hunters and later folk relying on rudimentary agriculture. Some of the Mesolithic flints from Great Parndon are shown in Fig. 2. These consist of a core from which blades have been struck, one of the blades, a waste fragment showing typically Mesolithic working and a minute blade, or 'microlith', trimmed to make a harpoon barb.

Fig. 2. Mesolithic flints
(Half actual size)

From this site has come a double ended burin, Fig. 3, which may be likened to a chisel or gouge. Burins were sharpened by the removal of fine splinters of flint and the arrows on the diagram show where such blows have been delivered. The Mesolithic people may have used pointed arrowheads, as very fine symmetrical flakes, Fig. 4, are occasionally found on their sites.

Figs. 3, 4. Mesolithic flints
(Half actual size)

This fine delicate material from Great Parndon is rather different from that of the valley Maglemosian sites and the nearest comparable material is that from High Beech. Similar sites occur all over Britain, especially on upland moors and very light soils, demonstrating the presence of hunting people, culturally adapted to light forest. All the Mesolithic sites in the area can be dated to somewhere between 6000 and 4000 B.C.

The presence of prehistoric material in the area of Great Parndon was known at the beginning of this century but this particular site was discovered a few years ago when a superbly worked flint projectile point, Fig. 5a, was picked up. It belongs to the Middle Neolithic period, about 2500 B.C., and is closely matched by another one from the Harlow Temple site by Harlow Mill Station. Fig. 5b.

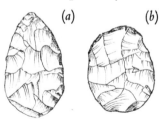

Fig. 5. Neolithic points, (a) Great
Parndon, (b) Harlow Temple site
(Half actual size)

Other carefully-made flints apparently made by the same people have been found at Parndon, including a projectile point only partially finished. These flints were probably left here by a group of people wandering south of their usual hunting grounds in Cambridgeshire and Suffolk where their large flint points are more usually found.

Polished axes of this period have been found in the Stort valley, one fine one being recently picked up at Sawbridgeworth.

Also from Sawbridgeworth, at Pishiobury, has come some distinctive Neolithic pottery known as 'Grooved ware'. This pottery was found in pits together with flints and bone points.

The period following the Neolithic phase is referred to as the Bronze Age, beginning about 1900 B.C. and lasting for approximately 1,300 years. Bronze was at first used only for prized weapons but gradually everyday objects were made from the new alloy. The later Bronze Age folk had the habit of cremating their dead and often placing the burnt remains in an urn which was then buried together with an offering or prized possession. The excavations at the Harlow Temple site uncovered the fragmentary remains of four or five funerary urns, Fig. 6.

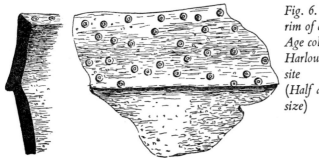

Fig. 6. Part of the rim of a Bronze Age collared urn, Harlow Temple site (Half actual size)

These Bronze Age urns were set in a line of pits but curiously enough, no bones were found inside them. A group of cremated bones was found, however, in a pit of its own. One vessel was not alone in its pit but was accompanied by a miniature flint axe, Fig. 7, perhaps a token object, in place of a real one far too valuable to bury in a grave. The shape of these 'collared' urns dates them broadly between 1400 and 1000 B.C.

Fig. 7. Very small flint axe accompanying a collared urn, Harlow Temple site (Half actual size)

Harlow is the site of several puzzling mounds. A group of these stand just to the east of the Princess Alexandra Hospital, another one is at Mulberry Green, and Canon Fisher records one at Netteswell. There may be the last remains of another on Latton Common. Until excavated it cannot be said for certain what these mounds really are. Probably they are barrows, or burial mounds of some period, although the possibility of their being ice houses cannot be ruled out. They may even be barrows converted into ice houses. Ice houses are hollowed out mounds in which in the late eighteenth century ice from the river would be packed in winter, and then covered with bracken and straw, for use later in the year.

The Hospital group of mounds is the most interesting and is sited by the side of Hamstel Road. The very fact that they occur in a line would suggest that they are barrows. Unfortunately, these mounds are very mutilated but the middle one appears to retain the original shape and would be the most rewarding of the three to excavate. Judgement on them must be reserved until excavation has taken place and all that can be said at present is that they are probably barrows, and, by their bowl shape, probably Bronze Age.

Some fragments of very coarse pottery, probably Bronze Age, have come from the Great Parndon site, but they possess no features from which to identify their style. The Late Bronze Age in the area is represented by several hoards of bronze objects. They appear to have been itinerant tinkers' stocks of metal and many of the objects are obsolete or broken implements which were presumably due for melting down. Hoards have been found at Arkesden, Ugley and Hatfield Forest but the most famous was found in 1893 near Colville Hall, White Roding. Most of the metal in this hoard consisted of worn socketed axes. Spearheads and harness trappings were also found. Of special interest were two handles belonging to a large cauldron. These hoards reveal to us the presence of warrior horsemen about 800 B.C.

In the second half of the first millennium B.C., successive waves of iron-using people came to Britain from the Continent and pottery of this period has been found from two sites at Harlow. The Great Parndon site has yielded a number of pottery fragments which show styles typical of both the early and late Iron Age. The evidence of constant occupation of this ideal site is most striking.

The other Iron Age site at Harlow lies beneath the Roman temple by Harlow Mill Station. As the finds are closely related to the Roman period in Gaul and Britain they are discussed in Chapter 2 in connection with the Roman material.

As may be seen from this brief account of the prehistoric period, remains of this phase in Harlow are not common, compared with many other regions in Britain. This is the case with Essex as a whole. The heavy clay soils had developed dense forests which were not extensively cleared until Saxon times when the region was settled on a permanent basis.

Chapter 2
Roman Harlow

Harlow lies near to the border between the territories originally occupied by the Belgic tribes known as the Catuvellauni, who lived mainly in the present county of Hertfordshire, and the Trinovantes of Essex. Before the Roman Conquest in A.D. 43, Cunobelin, after the death of Tasciovanus of St Albans, conquered the Trinovantes and moved his capital to Colchester. These tribes were the main enemies of the Romans in Britain but like all others they collapsed under the might of the legions. Once the conquest of the land had taken place their tribal centres became the principal provincial towns of Roman Britain.

There was probably a thriving community of Belgic people near Harlow during the century before the coming of the Romans, as indicated by the number of their coins found from time to time in the area. Although no settlements have been discovered they used a small hill, now known as Stanegrove or Standing Grove and situated about 250 yards west of Harlow Mill Railway Station, for their religious rites. At that time it is probable that the hill rose some 20 feet above the flood plain of the Stort and was partly surrounded by an ox-bow lake. Although it covered about ten acres, only the tree-covered top of the hill appears to have been used and it was to this sacred glade that the people came, performed their ceremonies and left their votive offerings, perhaps by hanging them on the branches of the trees or burying them in the ground. Recent excavations have defined a layer of soil which formed the original surface but which is now buried by up to 4 feet of accumulated debris and it is in this soil that the most important Belgic objects in the district have been found.

Twelve uninscribed gold coins lay within a limited area at the very top of the hill; they included two coins imported from the Continent, dated about 50 B.C. and probably reflecting Julius Caesar's conquests in Gaul, whilst others were probably minted in this country at a somewhat later date. They all bear the typical horse and wheel motif of early Celtic coins. Numerous inscribed bronze coins of Tasciovanus and Cunobelin were scattered over a wide area whilst coins from Leicestershire and Dorset indicate that the site was of sufficient importance to attract people from far afield. As the majority of Cunobelin's coins also bear the name of Tasciovanus it is probable that he wished the local population to understand that he was the rightful heir of their territory and it would appear that Harlow was politically closer to St Albans than to Colchester. Even before A.D. 43 the Roman influence was felt in

Essex; on some coins Cunobelin wears a laurel wreath whilst mytho-
logical creatures such as centaurs and griffins are illustrated frequently.
The importance of corn growing in Essex is indicated by the sheaf of
barley often found on British coins.

Bronze brooches of the first half of the first century A.D. were found
in such numbers as to suggest that they were left as votive offerings.
Although most were of simple design, others were elaborately decorated, sometimes with enamel in various colours. Occasional iron
brooches, bracelets of bronze and shale, finger rings, pins and toilet
articles were scattered over the whole area. Numerous fragments of
beakers, dishes, plates, flasks and bowls were found together with
quantities of bones of domestic animals, mostly of young sheep,
suggesting that the hilltop was occupied for considerable periods of
time although there is no evidence of any dwellings having been
erected. A number of holes, originally containing wooden posts, have
been discovered but they make no obvious pattern and their function
remains unknown.

Thus for many years before the Roman invasion, Harlow had been a
centre of some importance attracting even wealthy people from the
surrounding countryside to its little sacred hill by the Stort. There was
probably a settlement nearby but except for a scatter of Belgic pottery in
the marshland between the hill and the river and at Great Parndon,
evidence of occupation at this time has yet to be discovered.

With the Romanization of Southern Britain, Harlow reached even
greater importance. It lies within the triangle formed by three important
Roman roads—Ermine Street between London and Braughing, Stane
Street between Braughing and Colchester and the great military road
from London to Colchester. Many portions of a Roman road have been
traced from Braughing in a south-easterly direction passing near Much
Hadham and High Wych in a more or less straight line for about eight
miles but the last mile and the crossing of the Stort have not yet been
located. Traces of other roads in the district indicate that roads probably
ran toward Harlow from Epping and Great Dunmow.

As in earlier times Harlow remained a religious centre but there is
ample evidence of occupation in the neighbourhood dating from soon
after the Roman Conquest, although no actual town is known. At least
two villas probably existed within the area covered by the new town.
In 1953 building debris including a red cement floor and fragments of
marble were found over 6 feet below the present surface in a field just
north of Water Lane and not far from Tyler's Cross, where a rubbish
pit containing quantities of Romano-British pottery has been excavated.
More recently a large rubbish pit has been found in a private garden
at Felmongers. It was filled with masses of excellent pottery mostly of

the first century A.D. and included some beautiful examples of red Samian table ware imported from Gaul. Building rubble was present nearby but the actual foundations of the original Roman structure probably lie beneath the modern houses. However, it is fairly certain that a villa owned by a person of some wealth existed thereabouts. In 1940 enemy bombs on Bush Fair Common uncovered Romano-British jars, cooking pots and a storage vessel together with a plain Samian cup. In 1819 John Barnard stated that the foundations of walls, evidently Roman, had been seen about a mile north-east of Stanegrove, but their exact location remains unknown.

Numerous rubbish pits are said to have been observed in the region of Harlow Mill Station nearly all of which have produced potsherds mainly of native wares, and animal bones. A pit situated between the station and the bridge over the Stort contained first-century Belgic pottery and a spiral brooch dated to A.D. 90-110 whilst in the garden of a house in Priory Avenue considerable quantities of Romano-British pottery and Roman coins were found recently. Probably the best preserved structure was, unfortunately, completely destroyed in 1935 when a machine tool factory on the main road was extended and a complete tessellated mosaic pavement consisting of red, black and white tesserae set in concrete was uncovered. It measured about 14 feet in length and was 5 to 6 feet wide whilst there were probably wall foundations at one end. Some 60 feet south of this pavement a large square pit covered by a roughly circular mound was said to contain osseous powder, numerous potsherds and bronze or iron brooches and was presumed to represent a common grave. This is not far from the place where six wooden, dovetailed coffins were discovered about 2 feet below the surface when the Northern and Eastern Railway was constructed in 1841. Although the bones crumbled on exposure, between the knees of one skeleton was a fine earthen vessel resting upon a shallow dish whilst a flask had been placed near the head.

In this peaceful rural community the site of Stanegrove could develop unhindered. About A.D. 80 a temple of flint and mortar was constructed on the summit of the hill. The foundations of this building were recorded in 1764 and 1819 when it was thought that they represented one of a series of Roman stations or forts along the Stort valley between the territories of the Catuvellauni and the Trinovantes. The true character of the structure was not realised until it was excavated by Miller Christy in 1927 whilst the complete history of its building, its subsequent elaboration and its final decay were ultimately worked out in detail by yearly excavations conducted by the West Essex Archaeological Group between 1962 and 1968.

The earliest construction was that of a temple of conventional Romano-Celtic type with its entrance facing south-east. Such temples existed in Gaul and in Southern Britain where the remains of over forty have been recognized. Whilst some were within towns such as Caerwent, Silchester and St Albans, others were situated on hills apparently well away from any settlements as at Maiden Castle and Chanctonbury. In Essex there were five at Colchester, one at Gosbecks near Colchester and one at Great Chesterford in addition to that at Harlow. The Harlow temple was a comparatively simple structure consisting of a central shrine or cella about 25 feet square, with flint and mortar walls almost 3 feet thick and foundations up to 5 feet deep. This was surrounded by a veranda 12 feet wide bounded on the outside by a portico wall of dimensions similar to that of the cella. Very little of the actual walls remained, at most only two or three courses of flints being *in situ*. At the corners there was evidence of quoining with tile and the remains of the lowest tile course was still present in the cella wall. The floor had been made up by placing a thick layer of gravel directly upon the soil covering the hill but nowhere had the original floor surface survived. However, in the overlying debris, there were numerous tile tesserae each measuring about one cubic inch indicating that both cella and veranda had been floored with a red tessellated pavement. In addition, a few small, coloured mosaic tesserae were also found suggesting that a multicoloured mosaic, probably of small dimensions, had existed somewhere within the bounds of the temple. Quantities of wall plaster painted red, blue, green, yellow and white lay within and outside the walls. Not only had the temple been decorated inside but it appeared to have been plastered outside and painted in gay colours. Numerous roof tiles, nails and building debris were present over the whole site.

From the evidence of this and other excavations of similar structure and the study of better preserved temples in France, it is possible to produce a reasonable reconstruction. On such a plan there are of course a number of possibilities the most favoured of which is that there was a central square tower about 30 feet high capped by a gabled or pyramidal roof with high windows and a door in the centre of its south-east side. This was surrounded on all sides by a veranda roof 10 to 15 feet high supported by columns based on a low portico wall. Whilst there is little doubt that temples of this form existed on the Continent, it is perhaps more likely, in view of its exposed position and the solidity of the foundations of its outer wall, that the portico wall extended partly or wholly up to the veranda roof; certainly no portions of columns have been discovered at Harlow. Some people have suggested that the whole structure was covered by a single over-all roof or that the verandah was roofed leaving the cella open to the air. These theories

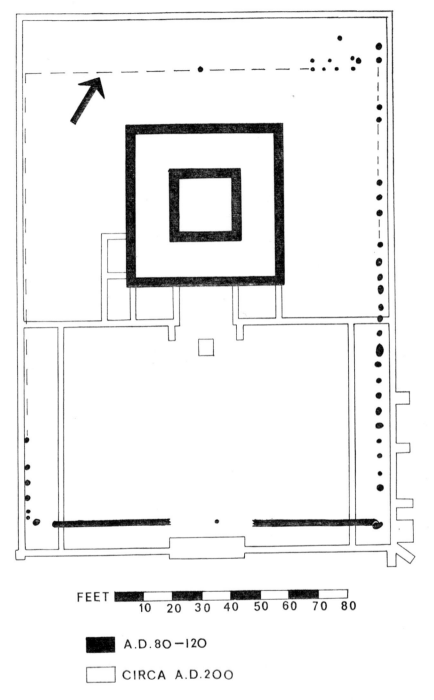

FEET

| 10 | 20 | 30 | 40 | 50 | 60 | 70 | 80 |

A.D. 80–120

CIRCA A.D. 200

Fig. 8. Plan of Romano-Celtic Temple

have been largely superseded in favour of the tower theory.

Contemporary with the building of the temple, graded flint pebbles had been placed directly upon the soil to form a well laid, cobbled surface extending over an area of at least 90 by 60 feet to the east of the temple and about 30 feet away from it. A bowl of Flavian date was sealed beneath the cobbles whilst coins of Claudius (A.D. 41–54), Nero (A.D. 54–68) and Vespasian (A.D. 69–79) were embedded between or lay immediately above them. In this area a shallow gully 30 feet long contained innumerable oyster shells.

If the cobbling had been intended to surround the temple, it was never completed for within a few years major improvements were made. Soil and the underlying gravel were removed from beside the temple and dumped over the ground to the south-east, covering the cobbles and producing a large flat surface around the temple.

This area was bounded on three sides by a pallisade of stout wooden posts and possibly by a low wall reinforced by wooden posts on the south-east side forming an enclosure measuring about 160 by 120 feet. The postholes for the pallisade on the north-east side were mostly about 21 inches in diameter, at least 2 feet deep and were evenly spaced at 5 foot intervals. At the north corner there was a complex of post-holes forming a structure of indeterminate nature. These were obviously later in date than the irregularly scattered postholes of the Belgic period described earlier. On the south-east side no postholes were found but the enclosure was marked by a linear foundation trench partly filled with glacial clay which could have supported a wall; this structure was lacking in the centre of the south-east side where there had probably been a gateway although conclusive evidence of its existence had been destroyed by later disturbance.

For perhaps a century the simple Romano-Celtic temple surrounded by its pallisade stood on Stanegrove whilst debris accumulated on its yellow gravel enclosure and the plaster weathered on its walls until about A.D. 200 when an elaborate reconstruction was undertaken preceded by a re-levelling of the area with clean gravel. Two symmetrical rooms each with internal measurements of 13 by 12 feet were attached to the south-east portico wall flanking a probable entrance to the veranda. Their walls were only about 2 feet thick and were plastered inside whilst a small portion of the original red tessellated floor remained.

Two small rooms were added to the south-west aspect of the temple. In front of the entrance was a square tile structure apparently representing a base for an altar, in the neighbourhood of which were large quantities of brightly coloured plaster and several fragments of tooled sandstone. A little distance away a piece of dressed sandstone inscribed

I The mootbury, or meeting hill, behind the Green Man, Old Harlow

II Mulberry Green, Old Harlow

III Excavation of Romano–Celtic Temple 1965. The foundations in the foreground probably supported a water-pipe and run diagonally across an earlier gully. Behind them is part of the outer wall of the later temple with the remains of a buttress

IV A selection of objects from the Romano–Celtic Temple site, of pre-temple date, including three gold coins, circa 50–40 B.C., three Cunobelin bronze coins, brooches of first half of first century A.D., toilet articles, finger ring and hairpins

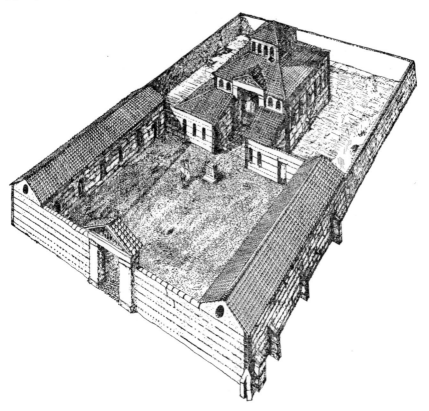

Fig. 9. Suggested reconstruction of Romano-Celtic Temple

with the letters NI.A was found; it appears to have come from an altar and may presumably be restored to read NUMINI.AUG.

A rectangular cobbled courtyard measuring 98 by 74 feet was made in front of the temple bounded on each side by a long room each with internal dimensions of 74 by 12 feet. The more easterly of these rooms was the better preserved and a considerable area of its red tessellated floor overlying a build-up of rubble collected on the site, had survived. It is possible that they were partitioned by light walls but flimsy evidence of only one possible cross wall has been found. The south-east boundary wall of the courtyard had originally stood at least 6 feet high and had a tile course between every three courses of flints. The central part of this wall was interrupted by the insertion of a flint and clay raft measuring 26 by 7 feet and 3 feet deep. A few mortared flints were present in one corner but otherwise the superstructure and most of the foundations had been removed during the seventeenth century. It was obvious that such foundations would have supported a substantial gateway but no evidence of its plan has remained. The rear temple enclosure wall was constructed of carefully laid flints forming a dry stone wall 2 feet wide on insubstantial foundations.

At a later date the north-east wall required additional support by a series of six buttresses but no further improvements were made to the building. It fell into decay or was destroyed during or after the reign of Constantine (A.D. 306–337). Many coins of this emperor were found in the superficial layers and were often covered by fallen walls or wall plaster. Thereafter the hill ceased to have any religious significance. Some temporary shelters and hearths were made amongst the ruins whilst in the Middle Ages and later most of the walls and their foundations were removed for buildings such as Latton church or for road construction.

Thus, in the Roman period one can visualize the gently sloping land between the tree-covered ridge of Rye Hill and the riverside marshes being covered by rough pastures in its upper region with cultivated fields below. The spur of higher ground at Old Harlow cut into the marshy strip to provide a natural river crossing near the temple which dominated the whole area beside the Stort. Here and there were villas modelled on Roman buildings and erected not for pleasure but as the homes of independent farmers. They ranged in size from cottage to mansion and were surrounded by farm buildings, servants' quarters and acreage according to their prosperity. In addition to these sumptuous dwellings it is probable that there were smallholdings consisting of groups of huts, corn drying ovens and storage pits with their accompanying arable land, occupied by natives who had not acquired the status, wealth and equipment of their neighbours.

Whilst the local agricultural produce would be sold at frequently held regional markets, the seasonal sale of animals demanded the provision of fairs which might attract people from a wide area and which, in the ancient world, were often associated with sanctuaries. It is not improbable that such fairs were held on Stanegrove within the shadow of the temple whose unknown deity ensured peaceful bargaining and hallowed the transaction.

Chapter 3
The Saxon Period

The period between the first coming of the Saxons and the Norman conquest covers about six centuries, and it was during this time that the area covered by the town and the surrounding district acquired—with small alterations—the village system which lasted until the development of the new town and the formation of the Harlow Urban District in 1955. Two notable events had their influence on the development of the countryside and the lives of the inhabitants—firstly, the conversion to Christianity, secondly, the coming of the Danes. The kingdom of Essex was first divided on a tribal basis, and a broad strip along the south bank of the Stort from Stane Street (now the A.120 running east from Bishop's Stortford) to the junction of the Stort with the Lea was occupied by one tribe; this became the Hundred (or Half-hundred as it was usually called) of Harlow, with its central meeting place at the 'mootbury' from which Mulberry Green takes its name. The Hundred was split up into smaller divisions consisting of groups of householders under a head man; these eventually became the villages. Two other important factors in the determination of the village areas were introduced by the Saxons—the heavy plough which was drawn by eight oxen, and the watermill. The great plough which was the basis of their agricultural system necessitated co-operative tillage, for only a man of wealth and importance would possess a full team of oxen.

The amount of land which a plough-team could keep under cultivation was called a hide, usually reckoned at 120 acres; a quarter of a hide was known as a virgate. To possess a virgate a family would have to own two oxen to make their fair contribution to the team, the holder of a half-virgate would have to own one. Virgaters and half-virgaters were the principal holders in a village. All our land measurements, field divisions, and tenures are based on the plough. The furlong, i.e. the length of a furrow, the distance the team could pull without a breather; the pole, i.e. the goad which could reach the leading oxen; the chain, i.e. the length of the plough chains; all are derived from this instrument and have given us in their turn the acre and rood as measurements of area. Large fields were necessary to get the best results from the heavy plough. For the mill some form of water-power was essential.

Mills figure prominently in the rolls and charters of this district. Before the Saxons settled here flour was ground by means of querns or hand-mills. These consisted of a circular stone trough or bowl in which another stone was revolved by means of an upright wooden handle placed eccentrically. The Saxons introduced the watermill and a number of these were established in the Stort Valley; within our area there were mills at Harlow, Latton, Gilston, Netteswell and Parndon.

To ensure for each village the requisites of large fields for tillage, and water power and also to provide a share in the woodland and commons, this district was divided into narrow strips, each having a mill-site on the river, with a portion of marshy meadowland. Above the marshes came a wide section of ploughland, and beyond that a strip of rough pasture rising to the woodlands of Rye Hill. The strangely elongated village areas (shown on the map at the back of the book), especially pronounced in the old parishes of Latton and Netteswell, were thus dictated by the needs of the villagers. On the most suitable site in each village, at a point in the arable belt where there was an adequate supply of water, the head man set up his abode, which in due time became the manor-house. All around were the great open fields. At some distance from this village-centre the villagers or townsmen, as they were called, constructed their rude dwellings at suitable spots by the cross-roads or adjoining the commons. In this part of Essex the open-field system seems to have broken down at a very early period; the small-holders continued to have their few strips, like large allotments, in a common field, but the more important tenants, the virgaters and half-virgaters, enclosed their land into small crofts grouped round their dwellings. Where the villagers' lands consisted of strips scattered over the wide open fields the homesteads were usually built in compact groups, forming a village nucleus; but where the land was enclosed, there was no such nucleus, the homesteads being dotted about all over the village area. This was very noticeable in Essex.

The principal tenants as we have seen were originally free co-operators in the working of the land, each providing his share of the plough-team, and each holding his proportionate number of acres. They were the men of the village, the townsmen (*villani*). Under pressure of circumstances, not least the Danish occupation, their status deteriorated, and they became villeins, still possessing an hereditary right to the land, but living under a heavy yoke and subject to many controls.

Before the spread of Christianity the principal unit was the family-group, which in later days was called the manor; as churches were built and manned a new division appeared—the parish. This might coincide with the manor, or it might embrace two or more manors. The parish seems to have been the final factor in determining the village area.

Although under the Saxons this area was mapped out and settled, they have left practically nothing in the way of ancient monuments or even stray relics of their occupation. Their buildings were primitive and

insubstantial, of wattle and daub or plain log huts. Not until the
Saxon era was nearing its end, when foreign influence had introduced
some knowledge of the arts, were buildings of a more permanent
character built in Essex.

The closing years of the Saxon period witnessed two important
events which were to have a marked influence on this area—the bequest
of Thurstan, and Earl Harold's foundation at Waltham. Thurstan, son
of Wine, was a Saxon thane owning wide estates in Norfolk, Cambridgeshire, and Essex. On his deathbed in 1041 he made extensive gifts
to a number of monasteries, some to take immediate effect, others con-
tingent on the death of his wife Ailid, for he had no son to succeed him.
To the great Abbey of St Edmunds he left his lordship of Harlow in
these words—'I give the land at Harlow to St Edmund's, except the
half-hide which Alfwine had at Gildenbridge,[1] and except the toft on
which Alfgar resides and the hoo thereto; and let all men be free'. This
is the earliest mention of Harlow that has come to light. Thurstan's
lordship was Harlowbury. The manor of Harlowbury was on the east
side of Old Road, Old Harlow, the present house having been erected
on the same site about 300 years ago.

About twenty years after Thurstan's death Earl Harold, son of
Godwin, founded a house in the forest at Waltham for secular canons.
Harold was no friend of the monks, but he was intrigued by the story
of the strange cross discovered in Somerset and miraculously brought to
Waltham, and he desired to enlarge the little shrine which had been set
up there and to endow it on a grand scale. He founded the house of
Waltham Holy Cross, not for monks, but for secular canons, i.e. clergy
living together under a common rule but each drawing his own income
and having some degree of independence. For the endowment of this
house he granted seventeen manors, mostly in Essex. One of these was
the manor of Netteswell, which stood to the west of St Andrew's
church in what is now termed Waterhouse Moor. The present farmhouse of Netteswellbury stands on the site.

Waltham Abbey has thus played an important part in the development of this town and since, as in the case of St Edmunds Abbey, many
records have survived, there is ample material to piece out the history of
these manors.

On the death of Edward the Confessor, Earl Harold was proclaimed
king, in accordance with Edward's last wishes and the people's desire,

---

[1] Gildenbridge appears as Ildenbridge in the thirteenth century, as Yeldenebrygge
in the fourteenth century, and was rebuilt in 1684 by the name of Yerlingbridge.
It was later corrupted to Ealing Bridge, and crosses Pinksey Brook on the boundary
of the parishes of Harlow and Sheering. It has given its name to Gilden Way, the
road which by-passes Old Harlow.

in defiance of the claims of William, Duke of Normandy. Preparations were made to set the country in a state of defence, while across the channel the duke was assembling his army, fitting out his transports, and awaiting a favourable wind. A close watch was kept along the Sussex coast and everywhere was tense expectation. Suddenly news was brought that a Norwegian fleet had landed an army on the Yorkshire coast. Harold made a hurried march to the north, gathering forces on the way, and decisively defeated the Norse invaders. Meanwhile the Norman host was at last able to make the channel crossing, and Harold was compelled to make another forced march to meet them. On his way south he stopped at Waltham, where he was joined by many of his former tenants, including no doubt some from this district. From Waltham, Harold, with such forces as he had been able to muster, marched to London and thence to the Sussex coast, only to fall at the battle of Hastings. With Harold's death the Saxon era closes.

Chapter 4
After the Conquest

The Norman conquest brought with it sweeping changes, but these mainly affected the wealthy landowners. William had invaded England with the Pope's blessing and although he made his brother Archbishop of Canterbury and gave several bishoprics to loyal followers, in the main he respected the rights of the church. Thus, most of the cathedrals and abbeys were left undisturbed in the possession of their estates, but all lay proprietors were deprived of their lands. For the lower grades of society the Norman conquest merely meant a change of masters, but the increased weight of taxation under the new regime gradually affected all ranks. To ascertain the taxability of the country William inaugurated a detailed and comprehensive survey. This was completed some twenty years after the King's accession, when the two volumes of Domesday Book were compiled. Domesday Book forms a bridge between the close of the Saxon era and the time when the Normans were firmly established in this land. It presents a separate survey for each county arranged not by parishes but under the headings of the principal land-owners, showing what manors they held in each Hundred. For each of these manors certain information was sought. Who owned it before the Conquest? What was its extent with the number of tenants and plough-teams? How much was it worth then? Who holds it now? What is its present state and value? Could this be increased? Within its limits Domesday Book is a veritable mine of information; its purpose was to establish a fair basis for taxation, and anything else was irrelevant.

The principal landowners at the time of the survey were five in number, owning estates in the parishes of Harlow, Latton, Netteswell and Parndon.

The monks of St Edmunds retained the manor of Harlowbury bequeathed them by Thurstan. In addition, William granted them three hides—approximately 360 acres—at Harlow and another estate at Latton. These were probably represented by Moor Hall, whose site is on the north side of the Harlow–Matching Tye road, about half a mile from its junction with the Sheering road; Hubbards Hall, lying to the south of St Mary and St Hugh's church, (Old) Harlow, and a Latton manor probably represented by Latton Priory, the ruins of which stand south of the town, west of the A.11.

Eustace, Earl of Boulogne, held the small manor of Kitchen Hall, now in the parish of Potter Street, where his tenant was Geoffrey de Mandeville, and also a manor in Latton where his tenant was Adelolf de

Merc who came from Marck near Calais and from whom it took its
name of Mark Hall. The site of this house is adjacent to the parish hall
of St Mary-at-Latton church in The Gowers. In Parndon he held the
principal manor, later known as Jerounds, where his tenant was Junain.
This manor, the site of which is north of St Mary's church at Great
Parndon and within the boundaries of the British Petroleum grounds at
Pinnacles, was held by the Whitsand or Wyssant family who took their
name from Wissant near Boulogne. Junain's full name was possibly
Junain de Wissant.

New Hall, (formerly Brendhall), which stands on the south side of
Gilden Way at the junction with Sheering Road, was granted to Eudo
Dapifer, steward to William, his tenant being named Turgis.

Peter de Valognes, brother-in-law to Eudo Dapifer, held a manor in
Latton, later known as Latton Hall, the site of this house and outbuildings being now called Cooks Spinney. His tenant was the Turgis of
New Hall already mentioned. The manor of Little Parndon, which
stood opposite the east end of the church of St Mary, Little Parndon,
and which was demolished a considerable time ago was also in the
possession of Peter de Valognes.

Two small manors in Great Parndon, Passmores and Canons, were,
according to the survey, granted to Ranulph, brother to Eustace, Earl
of Boulogne; he also held lands in Roydon which had attached to them
a holding in Harlow known as Welds, referred to in 1475 as Weldes and
Sewales, marked on the Chapman and André map (pages 88, 89) as
Saw Wells and now known as Sewalds Hall Farm.

Netteswell is totally omitted in the Domesday survey. Although
it belonged to the canons of Waltham Holy Cross before the Conquest
and was in their hands in the following century, there is no evidence to
show whether they remained in undisturbed possession. Unlike the
other religious houses Waltham was harshly treated by William, as
being the foundation of his rival Harold, and the canons were deprived
of much of their property. Eventually, however, the greater part was
restored to them, including most of their Essex manors, and amongst
them the manor of Netteswell. At the time of the survey the manor
may have been temporarily in the king's hands.

This then is the general picture of the area now covered by the town,
in the reign of the Conqueror. It will be seen that St Edmund's Abbey
not only remained in possession of the land bequeathed by Thurstan,
but was endowed with 3 more hides (360 acres) in Harlow and a rather
larger estate in Latton. In addition, it was rated at only $1\frac{1}{2}$ hides for
Harlowbury, although there were eight ploughs on the manor and its
value was given as £8. Taxation was based on hidage, so that this
manor, which in actual extent comprised 5 or 6 hides, was very

V The church of St Mary-at-Latton, from an old photograph

VI Club House, Canons Brook Golf Club, converted from an old farm building, standing on the site of the old manor of Canons

leniently assessed for taxation purposes. The larger manor at Latton (3½ hides) was valued at £6; it included a considerable area of woodland, sufficient for 200 swine. This manor is something of a mystery; none of the records of St Edmund's mention any property at Latton. It seems likely that at some time in the Norman period this estate was transferred to the Mark family and incorporated in their manor of Mark Hall.

For the century following the Domesday survey there is practically no documentary evidence, and the immediate successors of the first Norman landlords are uncertain. Of the state of the tenantry and any development in the villages we are left in ignorance. The opening years of the twelfth century, when Henry I was on the throne, were stable and peaceful. The chaotic years which followed during the struggle between Stephen and Matilda must have disturbed even this quiet backwater. Under Henry II there was a return to more settled conditions. It is at the close of his reign that we get a glimpse of the state of Harlow from a passage in the chronicle of Jocelin of Brakelond. Most of the large monasteries kept a chronicle in which matters of national interest were entered, but Jocelin's chronicle is unique in that it deals with the day-to-day affairs of the cloister. The central figure in his story is the Abbot Samson, who was confirmed in his office by Henry II in 1180. Soon after Samson's elevation the following incident is recorded:

'Once on a time, as we passed through the forest in returning from London, I inquired in the hearing of my lord abbot, from an old woman passing by, whose was this wood, and of what town, who was the lord, and who was the keeper? She answered that the wood belonged to the Abbot of St Edmund, as part of the town of Harlow, and that the name of the keeper was Arnold. When I inquired further, how Arnold conducted himself towards the men of the town, she answered, that he was a devil incarnate, an enemy of God, and one to flay the poor alive; but now, she added, he is afraid of the new Abbot of St Edmund, whom he believes to be prudent and vigilant, and therefore he treats the men gently. On hearing this, the abbot was delighted, and deferred taking to the manor for a season.'

Samson had found the finances of the abbey in a bad way. His predecessor had let out many of the manors on very unremunerative terms. One of the first acts of the new abbot was to revise these leases, and in most cases he took the manors into his own hand and farmed them through bailiffs. This he had intended to do at Harlow, but after hearing the report on Arnold he postponed the matter for a while. We shall hear more of Arnold de Harlow, but a word must be said about the forest.

The Norman kings were ardent hunters and large tracts of country were reserved as forest. Within these areas strict laws were enforced entailing much hardship on the villagers. One of the concessions made by Henry II at his coronation was a limitation of the forest areas, and the forest bounds were clearly defined. Under this measure the Hundred of Harlow was deemed entirely outside the forest, which stretched from the southern boundary of the Hundred to London and the Thames. This forest was generally known as the Forest of Waltham, but portions of it were often named from the nearest village. Samson and Jocelin had therefore left the forest by the time they reached Harlow, but the woodland and waste was of a similar character though it was actually outside the forest pale. They had come by the track-way which runs along Rye Hill and were passing the abbot's great wood of Harlow Park. This has now been partly deforested and lies at the rear of the nurseries of that name on the east side of the A.11.

The Norman era extends beyond the reigns of the Norman kings; it covers about a century and a half from the Conquest to the signing of Magna Carta. Its effect on the life of the country appears in the growing power of the church, the spread of monasticism, and the increased emphasis placed on the manor. The hall with its barns and buildings arranged round a court-yard became more and more the seat of authority. The manorial court supplanted the village moot, and the whole village population, freemen, villeins, cottagers, and serfs, found itself caught up in the toils of feudalism. The Normans were great builders. They adapted and improved the Romanesque style which they found in France and introduced it into this country. Many of their castles, churches, gateways, and bridges remain to this day, but few examples of domestic buildings have survived. The finest specimen of Norman architecture in our neighbourhood is the church of Waltham Abbey; actually within our town little of their work remains. The chapel at the gate of Harlowbury has a Norman doorway and in the much restored church of St Mary and St Hugh in Old Harlow the westernmost window of the north side is of the Norman period. At St Andrew's church, Netteswell, the inner arches of the doorways and the font-bowl are probably Norman.

The Norman builders found this district entirely lacking in building stone; for their walls they used rubble, but for quoins and surrounds they either had to import stone from a distance or else make use of the Roman bricks from the ruined Roman settlements. The south-east corner of the chancel of St Mary-at-Latton shows a quoin of Roman brick, possibly taken by the Norman builders from the Roman Temple or from a nearby Roman villa. In addition to these few relics of the Norman builders, some traces of their occupation can be discerned on the map of the district. The embanked fishponds at Netteswellbury (now Netteswell Pond just south of Second Avenue) date from the reconstitution of Waltham Abbey, when this chain of fish-stews was planned to supply the canon's table. In the reign of Richard I the canons of Waltham obtained licence to assart 40 acres of their wood at Netteswell, i.e. to stub up the trees, clear the ground and enclose it. On the slopes of Rye Hill this assart, known as the Riddens (or Riddings) remained a separate holding, complete with farm buildings but lacking a dwelling-house until recently. About the same date the abbey mill at Netteswell which for many centuries has borne the name of Burnt Mill, was being constructed. In the records of Waltham Abbey there is a series of charters dealing with this mill; in these, agreements were entered into with the lord of Gilston for the enlargement of the mill-pool and the control of the water. The Gilston mill seems to have been sited just to the east of where Harlow Town Station now stands, on the opposite bank, so close to Burnt Mill that the water-power was only sufficient for both mills by a mutual arrangement, and still leaving insufficient water-power for Parndon Mill. To increase the fall, Roger, son of Ambrose, the owner of Parndon Mill, agreed to pull his mill down and reconstruct it a furlong lower down the river.

Some Norman names appear from this period; besides Mark Hall, the manor of Passmores derives its name from a Norman occupier, Passemer. A document *circa* 1200 records a grant made by Southwark Priory to their porter Edmund of 8 acres at Parndon for an annual rent of 8d. This was part of the land which Passemer acknowledged to belong to the Priory. Around Netteswellbury a number of fields and a grove took their name from a family called Bray. In 1195 Sir Roger de Bray held this manor from the canons of Waltham and was followed by his eldest son Miles, but although their tenure only lasted a few years, such names as 'Great Brays', 'Little Brays', 'Brays Mead' and 'Brays Grove', are still in use. Towards the close of the twelfth century the Preceptory of the Knights Hospitallers at Little Maplestead was founded, and gifts of land and money flowed in from all over the county. Amongst the benefactors appear many from this town. Several members of the de Harlow and de Whitsand families contributed. Ambrose of Little Parndon and his son Robert gave to the Hospitallers, William the potter and his tenement; Robert and Roger de Parndon gave 3 acres in Southfield, and all the assart near their house; but most intriguing of all is the grant of Eutropius de Merk, lord of Mark Hall. He gave to the house of Little Maplestead an acre in Latton, 'viz. that acre over which Ailmar, the bishop, passed'. Ailmar was consecrated bishop of the South Saxons in 1009, and probably died in 1031; there is nothing to show what he was doing at Latton, or why the ground he walked over should be venerated nearly two centuries later. Some hidden story lies behind this benefaction. The Norman era ends at Runnymede, where King John was forced to sign the Great Charter by the champion of liberty, Robert Fitzwalter, lord of the manor of Roydon.

Chapter 5
Medieval Life

Little more than a year after the signing of Magna Carta King John died, and his young son Henry III came to the throne. During his minority an era of peace and prosperity set in. As the king grew older he dispensed with advisers and became more and more autocratic. Eventually he repudiated Magna Carta and claimed all the privileges which his ancestors had enjoyed. Amongst other unpopular acts he re-afforested the whole county of Essex south of Stane Street, thus bringing the Harlow Hundred within the forest pale. The struggle with the barons was resumed, at first disastrously, but with the escape of the young Prince Edward from captivity fortune favoured the royal party, and at Evesham the barons were decisively defeated. Henry's reign was, however, nearing its end, and when Edward came to the throne he was wise enough not only to renew the Great Charter and to restrict the forest areas to their ancient bounds but to give to the people a real share in the government of the country. His reign witnessed the birth of Parliament.

For the town of Harlow and the neighbouring parishes during the reigns of Henry III and Edward I there is considerable documentary evidence enabling us to trace the descent of the manors, and to learn something of the conditions under which the villagers lived. In the fourteenth and fifteenth centuries more records are available, and information is to be obtained from many sources, while in most cases the parish church with its monuments and inscriptions has some contributions to make.

The old town of Harlow at this period consisted of a cluster of houses around the church in Churchgate Street with Brendhall (New Hall) and its outer buildings just to the west along the present Sheering Road.

Another group of dwellings stood at Mulberry Green and possibly a few houses where Fore Street and Market Street now stand. South of Mulberry Green lay Hubbard's Hall with the home of Andrew le Yerdling beyond (later known as Old House) and finally Kitchen Hall at the edge of the common to the east of Potter Street.

Along Hoo Strate (Old Road) the principal road north, lay the abbot's manor of Harlowbury, and eastwards from Harlow standing away from the present Matching Green road stood the manor of Moor Hall.

The adjacent parish of Latton had Mark Hall and Latton Hall lying close to the church of St Mary. Southwards at Purfoots Green—now

Puffers Green, and from which the housing area of Purford Green is named—lay the village of Latton with some scattered tenements along the road to the common.

Netteswell, the parish adjoining Latton on the west, had its principal manor at Netteswellbury with two groups of houses at either end of the parish. At Netteswell Cross lay one group, with a house or two at what is now the junction of School Lane and First Avenue and the other to the south at Tye Green where possibly six houses lay.

At Little Parndon the manor lay close to the river opposite the church whilst a few tenements which constituted the village lay a mile or so south. On the higher ground still further to the south lay the principal manor of Great Parndon, on the north side of the church of St Mary, Great Parndon. On the south side of this church was another house later known as Catherines. Down by the present Cock Green was the village with a few scattered houses along the road leading south and east back to the commons.

This area in the thirteenth century consisted of five parishes, Harlow, Latton, Netteswell, Great and Little Parndon, the major part of which is now covered by the new town. The gentry then consisted of the lords of the manor, some holding in chief, others occupying the premises as tenants of some over-lord. In addition, there were a few substantial freeholders.

At (Old) Harlow the principal manor at this time was Harlowbury, held in chief by the abbots of St Edmunds. This manor was in the hands of Arnold de Harlow when Samson became Abbot and for a while he was allowed to retain it. The de Harlow's had evidently acquired control of much of Harlow by this time, but gradually the abbey, under Samson and his successors, began to regain control of its lands from the de Harlows. Arnold de Harlow appears on the Pipe Rolls from 1191 to 1194, and appears as a witness to several of Abbot Samson's charters. In the mid-thirteenth century Sir Richard de Harlow, grandson of Arnold's brother Ernulph de Harlow, ceded all claims to the manor and lordship of Harlow, also granting to Abbot Henry de Rushbrook (1235–1248) his windmill, and the multure of his tenants (i.e. the grinding of his tenants' corn), undertaking not to erect another rival mill on any part of his estate and to surrender all rights in any land at Harlow except his own patrimony of Moor Hall. Later, during the reign of Abbot Simon (1257–79) he ceded the right of common in the woods and pastures and a recognition that he owed suit of court, i.e. had to attend at the manor of Harlowbury, every three weeks.

In 1430, after a period of two centuries when the manor was farmed by the abbey through bailiffs, Abbot Curteys leased Harlowbury to

John Dobbs, and the inventory of the live and dead stock is preserved in the Harlow Cartulary. This inventory, described as an extent, was compiled in April, May, June and July 1431 in considerable detail and lists amongst many items fisheries, tolls of bridges and market, ways, paths and commons.

About a century later Giles Mallory held the lease and Thomas Cromwell, Henry VIII's chief minister, who wanted a residence near the king's new house at Hunsdon, sought to have the lease transferred to himself. An indenture was drawn up, but for some reason Cromwell changed his mind, and instead obtained a pension for himself and his son out of Harlowbury. At this time the monasteries were in danger of being suppressed and the abbot was no doubt anxious to appease Cromwell.

In 1536 Harlowbury was leased to William Sumner, whose brass effigy is on the north transept wall of St Mary and St Hugh's church, (Old) Harlow; and he continued as tenant after the Dissolution, when the estate was purchased by Lady Addington. The agreement between Sumner and the abbot is still extant, and helps us to picture Harlowbury as a typical medieval manor-house, with its great hall facing south into a courtyard. At the east end of the hall, separated by a screen and passage, was the kitchen; at the west end stood the parlour with one or more bedrooms above. Barns, stables, and outbuildings enclosed the court-yard. There may have been an outer as well as an inner court-yard, for an inquest held by the abbot in 1290 took place at the outer gate of his manor at Harlow. House and buildings alike seem to have been of timber and plaster, with roofs of tile and thatch, for the tenant was made responsible for tiling, thatching, claying, paling, gating, and walling, and was allowed to cut the necessary timber from the woods of the demesne. The only part of medieval Harlowbury still standing is the small Norman building near the entrance, and this appears to date from Abbot Samson's time. There is no reason to doubt that this was the manorial chapel standing by the outer gate; the position of the building and the materials used corroborate the traditional view. The manorial surveys show that besides the hall there were the usual manorial accessories, a mill, a dove-house, and an animal pound. There was a garden of 8 acres well planted with fruit trees, and a vinery and nuttery are specially mentioned. The mill was the present Harlow Mill Restaurant, (rebuilt in the seventeenth century), situated where the road to Sawbridgeworth crosses the Stort, the abbots claiming a penny toll from carts crossing the bridge by the mill.

The manor of Moor Hall, now outside the boundaries of the town but within the parish of Harlow, was held by Ernulph de Harlow. He was succeeded by his son, William, who died soon after 1235 and his grandson Sir Richard de Harlow who died in 1280. William and Richard figure largely in the various transactions between the abbots of St Edmunds and Harlow. Sir Richard was a staunch adherent of the king's party during the war with the barons, and suffered for his loyalty when Moor Hall was raided and his horses carried off. In 1268 he was sheriff of the county, and the king issued a writ for Colchester Castle to be delivered to him. Though he was twice married he left no son and heir. The next family connected with Moor Hall is that of Arderne. Ralph de Arderne appears in 1302, while in 1315 William de Arderne surrendered to Mathew de Wodeham, citizen of London, all claim he held in 'La Morehalle' in Harlow.

For the next 100 years the history of the manor is much confused, part of the lands being held by the abbot of St Edmunds, part by Lord Scales. To add to the confusion the manor was held in partnership and included lands in Sheering as well as in Harlow. At the inquisition after the death of Robert, Lord Scales, in 1324, Mathew Wodeham and John Snow were found to hold the tenure of the manor of 'Le Mour-hale' in Harlow. At the same time John Snow held a freehold in (Old) Harlow to which he gave the name of 'Snows'. This property later passed into the hands of the manor of Harlowbury, the tenure being held by Robert Bannister for a yearly rent of £5 10s 0d. 'Snows' was demolished in the early nineteenth century and when rebuilt was renamed The Wayre. It has now been purchased by the Urban District Council for conversion into flats for the elderly.

None of the inquisitions on later members of the Scales family mention Moor Hall, and in all the surveys of Harlow the name of Scales occurs once only, when a field on the Sheering road, just beyond Churchgate Street corner, was said to abut on the fee of Lord de Scales. This was a plough-land called Windmill Field, the site of Richard de Harlow's mill. Wodeham and Snow were also tenants of the abbot. In 1353 Wodeham's share was conveyed to Thomas Huberd. John Snow's portion passed to the Aylmers who held an estate in Sheering. In 1383 Robert Huberd and William Aylmer held equal shares in Moor Hall, but in 1409 Robert Huberd was the sole tenant.

In the survey for 1431, the Moor Hall section begins: 'William Rothwell, Esq., holds the moiety of a messuage formerly of Roger de Wodeham and the moiety of a messuage formerly of John Snow, now one complete messuage called Moorhall, lately of Robert Huberd, Esq.,' William Rothwell was a citizen and tailor of London. He bought the Huberd estates, Moor Hall, Hubbard's Hall, and Paris Hall from the trustees appointed under the will of Robert Huberd. From Rothwell, Moor Hall passed to the Bugges, who first appear at Harlow in 1433; they were the leading family in Harlow for the next two centuries, and are commemorated by brasses in Harlow church (St Mary and St Hugh's).

Hubbard's Hall, lying outside the eastern boundary of the town but within the parish of Harlow, was also dependant on Harlowbury; all three manors in the twelfth century were in the hands of the de Harlow family. Maurice de Harlow, who witnessed a deed of Abbot Anselm (1121–46), held Hubbard's Hall with special privileges and sporting rights over the abbot's lands at Harlow. These privileges Abbot Samson confirmed to Maurice's son William in 1182, and they were renewed to Hubert son of William. Hubert's heir, who always styled himself John Fitz-Hubert, was under age at his father's death, and was a ward of Simon de Luton, Abbot of St Edmunds. About the year 1270 there was a controversy between him and his former guardian, which resulted in his receiving a charter similar to that enjoyed by his father and ancestors. Hubbard's Hall was at this time a genuine manor, for the charter allowed the occupier to hold a court for his tenants. The sporting rights extended to all beasts and fowls of warren over all the abbot's lands at Harlow, and included a fishery on the Stort. John Fitz-Hubert's son and heir is styled John Huberd; from this time the surname became fixed after passing through a variety of spellings— Hubert, Huberd, Hoberd, and Hubbard. John Huberd was the most prominent member of the family, and from him the manor took its name. He was knighted, and held the office of coroner; he was also a verderer of the Forest of Essex. His name appears more than once in the Pleas of the Forest for poaching, and taking the king's deer. He died *c.* 1325, for on a taxation list for 1327 his widow Margery's name appears. In his later years Sir John Huberd became heavily in debt; one of his creditors was Sir Robert Fitzwalter, who owned the neighbouring manor of Welds. When Thomas Huberd succeeded to the manor he soon found himself in difficulties and engaged in a long lawsuit with Sir John, grandson of Robert Fitzwalter, who had distrained on the manor and carried off horses and oxen. Thomas Huberd's name appeared occasionally as a collector of wool for the district. He was succeeded by his nephew Robert, who on his death in 1428 left a widow and young children. Their guardian was their uncle, William Huberd, a London vintner, who contrary to the wishes expressed in his brother's will, sold the manor of Hubbard's Hall to William Rothwell. Rothwell sold the manor to Robert Symond. His grandson, also named Robert, was chief secretary to Henry VII for the Duchy of Lancaster; there used to be an inscription to his memory in St Mary and St Hugh's church, Old Harlow. Eventually, the manor passed with other property in the neighbourhood to the heirs of John Shaw or Shaa, Lord Mayor of London.

The manor of New Hall (Old Harlow) as we have seen was held at Domesday by Eudo Dapifer when it was called Brendhall. This means 'Burnt hall', a common enough occurrence when houses were of wood and thatch, and before brick chimneys were in use. From Eudo it passed through a succession of overlords until it escheated to the crown and became part of the Duchy of Lancaster. Under these overlords it was held by a Bedfordshire family called de Fletewic, who took their name from the village of Flitwick. Seven David de Fletewics in succession held the manor, but near the end of the reign of Edward III for want of a male heir the property descended to John Goderich, a Bedfordshire gentleman who married Eleanor Fletewick. Goderich appears to have sold Brendhall to William Bysmer, a London goldsmith, who held the manor in 1428.

Some time between 1435 and 1440 John Bugge, citizen and draper, purchased Brendhall. In the late fifteenth and early sixteenth centuries it was rebuilt in the prevailing Tudor style, when it received its present name of New Hall. Much of this work remains, although there have been later additions. The house was partially moated and had the usual manorial adjunct of a dove-house and an animal pound. John Bugge was the son of a London draper, and for some years acted as treasurer to Joan, Queen of England, the second wife of Henry IV. He was succeeded in 1442 by his son Stephen, who died in 1458, and his grandson Thomas. Thomas Bugge had also acquired the manor of Moor Hall, and as Kitchen Hall and New Hall were for many years held together, the family then owned three of the Harlow manors.

The small manor of Kitchen Hall was at Domesday held by Eustace, Earl of Boulogne. The name of this manor has always been somewhat of a puzzle. Morant's suggestion that it was derived from this manor supplying the abbot's table in accordance with a licence granted by Pope Boniface IX in 1398 may be dismissed. The manor never had any connection with the abbey, and the name occurs long before the time of Boniface. Manors were sometimes named from the material with which they were constructed or some prominent feature, e.g. Stone Hall, Shingle Hall, Copped Hall, etc., and possibly the kitchen chimney was the most conspicuous part of this hall, and gave it its distinctive name. A family named Fucher held this manor from the reign of Henry II until about 1260. William Fitz-Fucher appears c. 1190. His son, Nicholas, was a prominent figure during the first half of the thirteenth century. He was knighted, and for some time held the office of coroner. Henry Fitz-Fucher sought permission from the Abbot of St Edmunds, as patron of the church, to have a chapel on his manor, but there is no evidence to show that his request was granted. Had it been granted this would have given Potter Street and Foster Street a church nearly 600 years before the present building of St Mary Magdalene. During the Barons' War, the Earl of Gloucester's men seized Fucher's lands at Harlow, and under the Clares the manor was held by various tenants. In 1383 it was purchased by Robert Webb, citizen and mercer of London, who sold it in 1403 to John Roundell. Roundell's name is perpetuated by the housing area called 'Rundells', and also by a property in the southern portion of the old parish of Latton, now the home of an antique business on the A.11 which for centuries had been in the same ownership as Kitchen Hall. Kitchen Hall had a windmill on Harlow common which has long since disappeared, but which is mentioned in a deed of the year 1343 as 'Foucheres-melle', though the Fuchers' connection with Harlow had been severed many years earlier.

The two principal houses in the parish of Latton were the manors of Mark Hall and Latton Hall, the former occupied by the Merks. Eutropius de Merk flourished towards the end of the twelfth century. He was followed by his son, grandson, and great-grandson, all three named Henry. These were all well-known local personages, and under them the Mark Hall estate was improved and consolidated. Their wood on Rye Hill was emparked, and a small section of the Abbot of Waltham's wood adjoining the Riddens was included. The last Henry left no heir, and his widow married Elias de Colchester, who enjoyed the manor in right of his wife. Elias was followed by a series of different owners none of whom settled long at Latton. About the middle of the fifteenth century Mark Hall was held by Sir Peter de Arderne, chief Baron of the Exchequer, who founded a chantry in the church. Later the manor came into the hands of Sir John Shaw or Shaa, Lord Mayor of London, who as already stated had acquired Hubbard's Hall.

The Peter de Valognes referred to in the Domesday Survey held manors at Latton and Little Parndon, Sheering, and still larger estates in Hertfordshire. The Latton manor, later known as Latton Hall, was occupied under the Valognes by a family named de Latton. Gunnora de Valognes, great-granddaughter of the Domesday lord, married Robert Fitzwalter of Roydon and their daughter Christian married William de Mandeville, Earl of Essex. The Valognes manors in Latton and Little Parndon seem to have passed through Christian to her two daughters. Little Parndon fell to Lora and her husband Henry Balliol and Latton Hall to Isabell, wife of David Comyn.

The Balliols sold Little Parndon to the Benstead family; under the Comyn's Latton Hall was held by Sir Peter de Tany, lord of Eastwick and Stapleford. The de Tanys continued to hold Latton Hall until the early years of the fourteenth century. They played a bigger part in public affairs than the de Merks. Sir Peter was sheriff of Essex from 1236 to 1239, and his son Sir Richard held the same office in 1260 and 1261.

Under the tower of Eastwick church lies the cross-legged mail-clad effigy of a knight. There is no inscription and the arms on the shield are obliterated, but this is thought to be the tomb of Sir Peter de Tany. The Tanys were succeeded at Latton by a family named de Bibbesworth. Their chief estates were at Saling and Great Waltham, and they probably spent little time at Latton. During the latter part of the fifteenth century the tenants were of the Harper family. William Harper d. *c.* 1490 married the daughter of Sir Peter Arderne of Mark Hall. William and his wife and children are commemorated in a brass in St Mary-at-Latton church. A century later Latton Hall was in the hands of the Althams.

Netteswellbury granted by Harold to Waltham Abbey was held on lease in the reign of King John by the de Brays. Later it seems to have been retained by the canons and farmed through a bailiff until the Dissolution. There was, however, one property in the village at Tye Green which was usually held by a substantial tenant; this is Goldsmiths, sometimes referred to as Goldings. Roger de Netteswell held it *c.* 1200 and a few years later his son Thomas was the leading man in the village. Later in the thirteenth century it seems to have been the home of the de Dunmow family. In 1277 Richard de Dunmow was indicted in the Forest Pleas for keeping dogs and greyhounds without a licence, and a generation later Richard son of Simon de Dunmow was in trouble with the forest officials. Dr Reaney in *Essex Place-names* quotes an unpublished entry in the Court Rolls for 1465 'Goldsmiths anciently called Yorkes from Richard York, *c.* 1270'. In the fifteenth century most of the larger houses were acquired by London citizens: it was probably in this way that Goldsmiths got its name. In 1456 Katherine Otwey, widow of a London merchant, left a bequest to St Andrew's church, Netteswell. Her executor was her son-in-law, John Amadas, goldsmith. She probably lived at Goldsmiths. About the year 1500 another London merchant, Thomas Laurence, held Goldsmiths: he is commemorated by a brass in St Andrew's church, Netteswell. Another holding at Tye Green is Jean's Yerdling or Yardling, (John's Virgate), which the de Dunmow family may have held from the Yorkes. In the *Deanery of Harlow* Canon Fisher quotes a document from the Waltham Cartulary (Harl.MS.4809) which runs 'To all Christ's faithful who shall see or hear the present writing, John, chaplain of Netteswell, gives greeting. You will have known that I have given and confirmed to God and the church of Holy Cross at Waltham, and to the Canons serving God there, one virgate of land and its appurtenances, which formerly I used to hold of their will and permission in Netteswell, as right belonging to the church of Waltham. Witnesses, Geoffrey, prior of Latton, etc.' John was chaplain of St

Brass lying in the Chancel of St Andrew, Netteswell. 'Here lyeth
Thomas Laurence and Alys his wife which Thomas decessid y^e xxiiij day
of April MDXXII, on whose soule Jesu have mercy.'

The brass represents a civilian and wife in the typical costume of the
reign of Henry VIII, the wife with a flat kerchief by way of head-dress.
Below are portrayed their two sons and five daughters

Andrew's church, Netteswell, in the early thirteenth century.

At Little Parndon, under the Valognes family and later the Bensteads, the manor was held by a family who took their name from the village. Mention has been made of Ambrose of Little Parndon in connection with the mill, and also his son Roger. Roger de Parndon Parva (or de Perendune) changed his name to de la Mare, and a long succession of de la Mares enjoyed the manor of Little Parndon. The railway has disturbed part of the site of their manor house by the river, but a good deal of the moated enclosure exists between the railway and the river, the site of the house being just east of the church.

At Great Parndon the principal manor was held for about two centuries by the Whitsands, descended from a follower of Earl Eustace of Boulogne. Richard de Whitsand was sheriff in 1250. He died three years later and was followed by his son Baldwin. Baldwin de Whitsand had three daughters, and on his death the manor and the advowson of the church were divided between them. Agnes, the eldest daughter, married Walter Geround. Their manor-house, called 'Gerounds' or 'Jerounds', which as already mentioned stood on the north side of the church has long since disappeared. Lucy, the second daughter, married John de Winton; they set up their manor-house to the south-east of the church. Their daughter Katherine, who married John de London, enjoyed this manor for several years, and from her it is still known as 'Catherines'. She left no heir; so this portion escheated to the crown, and was granted to Waltham Abbey. The third daughter, Elizabeth, married Taylifer, brother of John de Winton. Her portion, called 'Taylifers', passed through various hands till it came into the possession of John Steward, *c.* 1385. The Steward family owned it for several generations, and the house, which lies north of Commonside Road, near to the Chequers Inn, retains the name 'Stewards'. The manors were later amalgamated, but the advowson was until recently divided into three parts, three different patrons each in their turn appointing the rector of the parish. At Catherines most of the house is of early seventeenth century construction, but at the eastern end there are some interesting remains including a painted wooden ceiling, of a much earlier manor-house dating from *c.* 1400.

These were the principal gentry in the middle ages, and their names constantly occurred when any enquiry was held or some transaction witnessed. Most of them had estates elsewhere, and in the management of their various properties, in public business, in sport, and from time to time in arms, their time was well occupied. Their domestic arrangements were primitive; the typical manor-house consisted of one large room, the hall, with a parlour and bedroom at one end, and the kitchens and store-rooms at the other. But though the gentry lived in considerable discomfort, they were well fed and had plenty of opportunities to travel. Wills of the fourteenth century show that some of the lesser known gentry also held tenements and land in London and Epping. Walter de Herlowe in his will of 1327 left a tenement in All Hallows, London Wall and land in Epping. In 1329 Nicholas de Perundune (Parndon) left a shop and brewhouse in the parish of St Nicholas de Colemanstrete, two shops in Spitelstrate and 10 acres of land in Parndon. Richard atte wood, de Harlowe, d. 1361, left a house known as 'Redebachous' in St Clements Lane to Sir John Clobbe, chaplain; William Aylmer; Walter Campioun; and John Page. The Aylmers held Moor Hall and Walter Campioun lived on the Sheering Road.

The life of the villager on the other hand was very circumscribed, and he had little liberty of movement or action. His small farm, a score of acres or so, was held at the will of the lord. For this he rendered certain services laid down by custom, and as long as these were paid he could not be dispossessed. His holding passed at his death to his lawful heirs, but the heir had to pay a fine on taking possession, and usually the lord claimed one of the late tenant's beasts or belongings as a heriot, a sort of death duty. The services paid to the lord might include a money-rent but were mainly manual tasks. The medieval manorial surveys give a list of all the tenants and lay down the services due from each of them. Though the details vary from manor to manor, some being much more exacting than others, we can get from them a fair picture of what a holder of a virgate or half-virgate was expected to do.

One of the Waltham Abbey registers contains a very early series of surveys which may be dated 1230–35. At Netteswell the tenantry were dealt with house by house irrespective of the size of the holdings; the surveyor had evidently started at the north-west, where the road enters the village from Parndon, and finished at the south-east, where the road along the common leads to Potter Street. Richard, the ploughman, was the first substantial tenant on the list; he lived at The Dashes, Netteswell Cross, and held a half-virgate, or 15 acres. For this he paid no money-rent but he gave a cock and a hen one year, a hen only the next year, and fifteen eggs annually at Easter. He worked for the lord on Monday, Wednesday, and Friday one week, and on Tuesday and Thursday the next week, throughout the year, except on feast-days. In addition, he did various extra tasks of ploughing, harrowing, and hay-making at the lord's request. These were called boon-works, and though they sound optional were none the less compulsory. As some compensation the lord provided food on these occasions—bread, ale, soup, 'companage', and cheese. 'Companage' is a word for which there is no exact English equivalent; it means something to spread on bread. The tasks at the manor included work of all kinds, threshing, hoeing, carrying wood or dung, carting corn and hay, indeed anything which the bailiff or reeve might require. Some tenants were liable to more distant carrying service up to twenty miles or so. All were bidden to come for the nut-gathering, either up to noon without food, or till the evening with food from the lord. Another tenant, William of Warley, 'holds 5 acres and a messuage for a rent of 22½d, he stacks hay and otherwise does like Ingeleyt, except that he does not mow'.

One of the St Edmund's registers gives us the services of a virgater at Harlow in 1287. Andrew le Yerdlyng (i.e. 'the virgater') held one virgate, and worked from Michaelmas to the fortnight before August 1 four days a week, viz. Monday, Tuesday, Wednesday, and Friday, except on feast-days, and except in the weeks following Christmas, Easter, and Whitsunday. Besides the usual farm-tasks he might be called on to carry as far as Stapleford (where the abbey had another manor) or to Bishop's Stortford, Waltham, or Ongar. He might even have to go as far as London, in which case he was allowed a white loaf, a dish of meat, and ale. From the fortnight preceding August up to Michaelmas he had to reap and harvest 18 acres. Andrew was also liable for boon-works, and for these he was well fed, receiving at noon soup, bacon, cheese, and ale, and in the evening, wheaten bread, two dishes of meat, and ale. Amongst the tasks he might be called upon to do were thatching, draining, folding, carrying dung to the ploughlands, and carting brushwood from the lord's park to the manor. His works were all priced, suggesting that the tenant might compound for a money payment. He paid no money rent, but gave a cock and hen at Christmas (worth 2½d) and thirty eggs (worth 1d). He might graze a pig in the lord's field (i.e. after the harvest) for 1d or a piglet for ½d. If he attended the Helymote (i.e. the manorial court), or the Hundred court, on a working day he was excused his task.

At first sight it would seem that a virgater could not possibly render all these services and work his holding as well. But it must be remembered that his day-work usually ended at noon, and in most cases there would be several members in a household, only one of whom would be called on to work at the manor. In practice the laziest or weakest member was sent. There was, too, always a supply of hired labour from the ranks of the small-holders and cottagers.

Apart from the exacting services required of him the villager suffered from many restrictions, and his life was for the most part confined to the village. He could not marry, or give his daughter in marriage, without the lord's permission. He could not sell his stock without the lord's permission, nor let off a piece of his land, nor could any of the family go to reside outside the manor. He could not have his corn ground at anyone else's mill, nor let any of his straw or the produce of

VII The chapel of the manor of Harlowbury, standing to east of the Old Road

VIII The mill at Little Parndon

his land go outside the manor, nor alter a boundary or cut down a tree. For all these things the lord's permission could be obtained at a price. He had to attend the manor-court and 'the View'. This latter was not a manorial function, but was frequently delegated to lords of the manor of high standing. It was in the nature of a muster or inspection, and dealt with various petty offences. For this muster all the male villagers over the age of twelve were arranged in groups of ten, called tithings, each represented by their head-man. A tithing was liable for any crime committed by one of its members. It was usually at the View that offences by bakers and brewers were dealt with. The village inn and the village shop had not yet become regular institutions. All the villagers were engaged in agriculture, but many of them had an additional occupation as butcher, smith, carpenter, weaver, dyer, etc., while their wives baked and brewed. Baking and brewing were liable to inspection, and local officers were annually appointed in each village to see that bread and ale were up to standard. It must have been very irksome for these officers to visit every house where baking and brewing for sale was going on, and almost every court roll records that the ale-taster had neglected his duty. The earliest extant Essex court roll is a Waltham Abbey roll for the year 1269. It records the transactions at a series of courts held that year on their various manors; at some of these bakers were fined for selling bread under weight and unstamped.

Offences frequently presented at the courts were blocked ditches, straying cattle, defective buildings, encroachments, cutting down trees or brushwood and causing obstructions in the public ways. For all these delinquencies fines were inflicted and the offender was ordered to make good whatever was amiss. What with his tasks, his restrictions, and his fines, one might think the villager's lot was a very hard one; nevertheless he enjoyed many advantages—not least, security. He lived in a well-ordered and strictly controlled society. He could not be dispossessed, and could pass on his land and belongings to his heir. He was protected against damage of all kinds such as robbery, trespass, or a slovenly neighbour. He was reasonably assured that any food or drink he might buy would be up to standard. He shared various benefits with other tenants of the manor—the right to graze his beasts on the common and on the stubbles and to let his pigs run in the woods, the right to dig turf for his fire, and to take a limited amount of timber and brushwood to repair his home and his implements, the right to sue a neighbour for debt or damage and to know that justice would be done. He had his recreation too, but like everything else this was controlled. Market and fair-days brought some variety into his life. A medieval village was very self-contained and almost self-supporting, but some medium was necessary for disposing of surplus goods and supplying simple needs.

Hence from very early times markets grew up at convenient centres facilitating interchange of produce, while the fairs which were held at less frequent intervals offered an opportunity for the sale of cattle and the purchase of articles not obtainable in a village. The privilege of holding markets and fairs was granted to certain lords by royal patent. Harlow market, which in its early days was held where the Chipping-field houses now stand, and later in Market Street, is mentioned in the reign of King Stephen, and may have been in existence long before that date. In 1218, Abbot Hugh, who succeeded Samson at St Edmunds, obtained from the child King Henry III the grant of a weekly market at Harlow to be held on Mondays and an annual fair to be held for two days on 'Christmas and its morrow'. In 1449 Henry VI renewed this grant with some alterations—the market-day was changed to Friday, and instead of the Christmas fair two new fairs were instituted, one on May 31 to commemorate St Petronilla to whom a chantry in the church had been founded, the other on November 17, the feast of St Hugh, one of the saints to whom the church of St Mary and St Hugh, Old Harlow, is dedicated. The former fair was mainly for the sale of wool, the latter for horses and cattle. The site of the fair-ground is now occupied by Barclay's Bank and the neighbouring premises in Station Road. Much more important than either of these was the great fair later known as Bush Fair, held by virtue of a grant to Latton Priory; this was held on Latton Common on the feast of the beheading of St John the Baptist (August 29) and the day following, for the priory was dedicated to St John the Baptist. This was a very large and popular fair and served a wide neighbourhood. Both the *Essex Review* (Vol. xliv, page 78) and *White's Directory* state that Bush Fair was held on September 9, i.e. a discrepancy of eleven days compared with the date in the earlier reports. This discrepancy is probably accounted for by the introduction of the Gregorian Calendar into this country in September 1752, when Wednesday, September 2, was immediately followed by Thursday, September 14, and led to the outcry 'give us back our eleven days'. This change of calendar would have altered August 29 to September 9 for the years following 1752. Bush Fair had been a general fair supplying all kinds of commodities, but in later times was principally a cattle fair also frequented for pleasure purposes.

Besides the markets and fairs there were the church's festivals and saints' days to make a welcome break in the lives of the villagers; indeed the church provided the peasantry with most of their interests and entertainments, and brought some colour into their lives.

With the dawn of the fourteenth century villenage which was the core of the manorial system began to break down, two outstanding events hastening the decline. The first of these was the Black Death, an epidemic of unparalleled virulence which reached England from the continent towards the end of 1348, and had spread to the central portion of Essex by May, 1349. No contemporary records for this town have been preserved, but court rolls from the Rodings, Blackmore, etc., are extant, and give some idea of the mortality in the neighbourhood. The courts were only concerned with tenants, no notice being taken of anyone not holding some property from the lord of the manor. At one manor at Blackmore embracing about half the village which had a population of perhaps 400, no less than 70 tenants died in May and June of that black year. Taking quite a conservative estimate it is probable that at least a third of the population of the county perished of the plague. In many cases whole families died out, and none was left to inherit their holdings. Consequently the old system was disrupted; many properties remained in the lord's hand, and were eventually let out at money rents. There were several recurrences of the epidemic, 1362 being another bad year in Essex. Meanwhile the long-drawn-out campaigns in France had added to the burden of taxation, and disbanded soldiers returned from the wars did much to disturb the countryside. Scarcity of labour had given the villein new importance and a desire for more freedom. Thus many factors were at work to upset the old manorial economy. In 1381 these various undercurrents came to a head in the peasants' revolt, commonly known as Wat Tyler's Rebellion, but invariably referred to in contemporary records as the 'tempus rumoris'. This town was certainly involved, though the chief disturbances took place along the line of the great Essex road from London to Colchester. The peasants thought that by destroying all records the manorial system would be put out of gear. In every manorhouse there was a double-locked chest in which the manorial rolls were stored in leather bags. Bands of peasants stormed the manors, rifled the chests, and burned the rolls. As the result for many Essex manors, as at Harlowbury, the manorial records only date back to 1382, and whenever this is the case, we can guess that the rebels had visited that manor. For this town only one small Waltham Abbey court roll covering the years 1269, 1270 has survived. The next extant Waltham roll is for the year 1400.

The revolt was crushed and stern efforts were made to fix wages at a low figure, and to exact all the old manorial services; but economic laws proved inexorable. There was a steady leakage from the countryside to the towns, and it was found impossible to restore the manorial system on its old footing. Custom, however, is strong, and the peculiar customs of each manor persisted for a long time in name at least, though the status of the tenants had materially changed for the better.

Throughout the middle ages this district supplied most of its own requirements; such commodities as were not grown or made locally were usually obtained at the great fairs. The largest and most celebrated fair in East Anglia was Sturbridge fair held just outside Cambridge on the road to Newmarket. Here such household necessities as salt and stock-fish were bought, wine and spices, besides luxuries such as silks, velvet, and furs. Everything could be obtained at Sturbridge, and though owing to the growth of the towns and better-class shops the fair declined in importance it was still a busy mart in the seventeenth century. The Latton burial register for 1624 records the death of a Londoner at Potter Street as he was returning from Sturbridge fair in September. Harlow Bush Fair was not on the same scale, but it was a large and busy fair, and served a wide district.

Harlow market had never been in a flourishing state; it seems to have lapsed altogether in Tudor times and is last mentioned in 1554; Norden, who wrote in 1594, does not include it in his list of Essex markets, and it certainly was not functioning in the seventeenth and eighteenth centuries. An effort was made to re-establish the market in the early part of the nineteenth century when a certain amount of development was taking place in the neighbourhood. A plan of Harlow in the year 1825 indicates a market-house opposite the Crown; this was probably erected when the market was revived. The market was held on Wednesdays, and continued for several years; but there were too many rival markets in the neighbourhood, and Harlow was not the centre of a sufficiently large district to support a market of its own. *White's Directory* for 1848 says 'The market, held on Wednesday, has been revived, but is of small importance'. It lingered on for a few years, and was then finally abandoned.

Chapter 6
A Fifteenth-Century Survey

The close of the medieval period is a good time to take a survey of this district, and to see how far the general layout has been altered in later days. For the greater part of Harlow, extents were drawn up for the Abbots of St Edmunds in 1383, 1410 and 1431, the originals of which are contained in the Harlow Cartulary, now in the Cambridge University Library. These were compiled in great detail, and enable us to locate all the tenants and their holdings. An estate-map made for Sir Edward Altham, the lord of Mark Hall, in 1616 covers the whole of Latton and part of Harlow (see page 54), while maps of later date (see Chapman and André map, pages 88, 89) show what changes have taken place in Netteswell and Parndon. The canalization of the Stort and the construction of the railway have altered the appearance of the river valley which bounds the town on the north, and have obscured such medieval features as the meadow-strips attached to the villein-holdings, but the mills and mill-pools have hardly been disturbed.

The roads of this period, with certain exceptions, have either become metalled roads, or have degenerated into bridle paths, or have been incorporated into the cycle track system. Latton Street which runs from its junction with the old A.11 at Potter Street through Mark Hall South and North to the old Netteswell Road is now a cycle track. The Harlow–Netteswell–Parndon Road is still part a road (Park Hill and part of Park Lane) and part cycle track, with the portion in what is now the Wych Elm area re-aligned to allow the building of the Telephone Exchange and the buildings westward of it. The Netteswell road from Netteswell Cross to Tye Green and the commons is represented today by School Lane to Broadfield School and then disappears under the new road system to re-emerge as a cycle track near Netteswellbury Farm running south to Tye Green Village where the old road through the village to Southern Way is still in use. Many of the old green lanes and bridleways of this period (such as parts of Commonside Road, and Peldon Road) still exist in parts, but the greater portions have disappeared under bricks and mortar.

The medieval surveyors who drew up the extents of the manor of Harlow divided the town into streets (*vici*) or wards; these were nine in number, viz. Hoo Street (Old Road), Moteburgh Street (the Sheering Road from Mulberry Green to Churchgate Street), Yeldenbregge (Ealing Bridge), Moor Hall (now demolished), Harlow Tye, Churchgate Street, Foster Street, Potter Street, and the market (Fore

Part of an estate map made for Sir Edward Altham, the lord of Mark Hall, in 1616

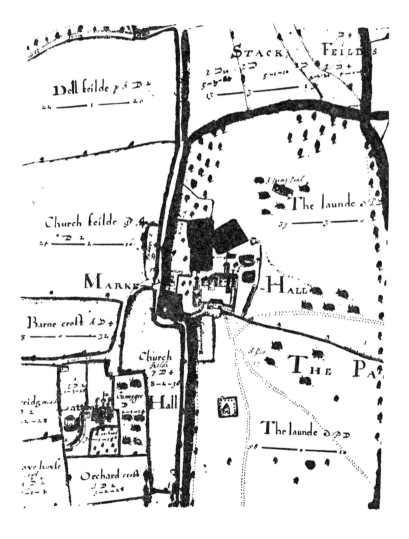

Street and Market Street, Old Harlow). All these names are still in use in some form or other, except Hoo Street (though the name 'The Hoo' has been applied to a housing area near Harlow Mill Station).

A traveller approaching Old Harlow from the north would cross the river Stort by the mill-bridge and then proceed up Hoo Street (Old Road), which ran from the mill to Mulberry Green. On the left near the river stood a villein-holding called Razoures: on either side of the road lay large plough-fields belonging to the demesne. About halfway along the street on the left was the entrance to the manor of Harlow-bury, with the old Norman chapel standing beside the outer gate. At Mulberry Green the road bearing to the left was called Moteburgh Street (i.e. the street of the meeting-hill). Mulberry is a modern corruption of Moteburgh; the hill lies behind the present Mulberry Green House and to the south of Gilden Way, and is reached by a track which formed a continuation of Hoo Street. Moteburgh Street ran from the green to Churchgate Street corner, but the eastern section between the ford (which existed where the new Gilden Way crosses the old road) and the corner was sometimes called Church Street.

Along this road were a few tenements, and on the right just before reaching the ford, stood the manor of Brendhall or New Hall, with its animal pound on the roadside near the gateway. The street passed through the brook by the ford, but there was a wooden bridge for pedestrians, this being replaced by a road bridge in 1904. Beyond the ford was the entrance to the vicarage. A little further eastwards the road divided, bearing left to Sheering and straight on to Matching; nearby another track turning sharper to the left led down to the meadows, so that four roads met at this point (a road pattern which still exists). The junction of these roads was called the Weylate, a common Essex term for a cross-roads. The Sheering road from the Weylate to the brook which divides Harlow from Sheering was called Yeldenbregge, taking its name from the bridge which crosses the stream and which is known as Ealing Bridge. The chief property in this quarter was a freehold estate, which in the thirteenth century was called Gobions. In the disturbed time of the barons' war this property was wrested from William Gobion by the Earl of Gloucester. From about 1300 until at least 1549 a family named Campion held this estate, which still bears their name. In 1441 Campions was broken into by thieves, who wounded John Campion and escaped with their plunder. The stolen property included a quantity of household linen, a scarlet gown trimmed with fur, and £10 in cash, indicating that Campion was a man of some substance.

The Matching Green road was called Moor Hall Street; it passed the manor of Moor Hall on the left. Behind the manor house the lands sloped down to the Pinksey Brook, where the marshes were known as

Harlow Moors. To most people moors probably suggest hills and heather, but in Essex the word indicates wet boggy pastures; it is derived from the Saxon word mor, meaning pool.

South of Moor Hall Street and reached from it by a lane, is Harlow Tye. Tye means a small piece of land, often as here where three roads meet. Round the Tye stood four villein tenements, Heywards, Mores, Tyes and Jackets; east of the Tye was a field called Chiswick, a name occurring frequently in Essex and signifying a cheese-dairy. Cheese was largely made from the milk of ewes, and the dairies were set up near the sheep pastures. A lane running westwards from the Tye joined Churchgate Street at Hobbs Cross.

The Churchgate Street ward included the short piece of the Sheering road from Churchgate Street to the Weylate, and the whole length of the road from the corner of Hobbs Cross. The first house on the left in Churchgate Street, where Meadham now stands, was called 'the old vicarage', and had been the vicar's residence in the days when the parish was served by both a rector and a vicar. After the rectory was appropriated to St Edmunds Abbey, the living became a vicarage only, and the vicar was granted the old rectory-house which stood on the northwest of the church. But for many years afterwards the house at Churchgate Street corner was known as the old vicarage; in a deed of the year 1582 it is described as 'le old vicaredge'. A little beyond this house is a lane which used to lead to the Moor Hall windmill and which is still called Mill Lane. On the west side of the street near the present Harlow Churchgate C. of E. School was the residence of the chantry-priest, and it was here no doubt that he taught his school.

Beyond the church gates was the house of the vicar's chaplain, and close to it dwelt the church-clerk. Further on stood the small dwelling with its outhouses and closes from which the chantry-priest derived part of his stipend, and where at first the chaplains of the chantry had their residence. The site is now occupied by the Churchgate Hotel (formerly the Chantry House). This house is an interesting specimen of Jacobean architecture, built after the chantry was dissolved. Recent additions were made when it became a hotel.

Beyond the Churchgate Hotel the street was called Watery Lane; here a brook running along the eastern side of the street frequently overflowed the roadway and made it a very miry way. The brook flowed over the road in the dip near the Churchgate Hotel and then ran westwards bounding the vicarage lands. Close to the water-splash another way from Harlow Common behind Churchgate Hotel joined Churchgate Street; at the junction of these ways a wooden bridge used to span the brook, and taking its name from St Petronilla, the chantry saint, was called Parnelsbregge, Parnel being the popular form of

Petronilla. This bridge was the cause of much controversy; the vicar of Harlow was responsible for its maintenance, a duty he frequently neglected. In 1418 John Dygge, the vicar, was presented before the Hundred court at Harlow for allowing this bridge to fall into a ruinous condition, whereas it was stated that it ought to be strong enough to bear four men carrying a corpse to the churchyard.

Along the left side of the road going to Hobbs Cross several villein holdings were grouped. Bridges, Hacches, and Goldyngs lay close together; next came a freehold called Franklins, and then Hills and Gowynes. Franklins, rebuilt at a somewhat later date, is still standing; for several generations it was held by a family named Franklin (i.e. the freeman). Eustace le Franklin lived here in 1200. In 1247 Geoffrey le Franklin was killed one evening as he stood at his gate by William son of Thomas; the murderer escaped, so the vill of Harlow had to pay the heavy murder fine. Later the house was occupied by a family named Haver and it was John Haver who rebuilt it. On a beam in the living room is this inscription: 'JOHN HAV' ANNO DOMENOE 1583'.

At Hobbs Cross the road forks left to the Lavers and right by Foster Street to the common. The road to the Lavers was in medieval times called Triste Street. At the cross roads in the village now called Threshers Bush a tree protected by palings marks the site of the old landmark of this name; it appears in an eighteenth century deed as Tricers Bush, which links up with the ancient name of the street. Triste is only another form of 'tryst', an appointed meeting-place. Triste Bush was a meeting place for the chase; in former days land may have been held by the service of bringing a couple of hounds to this spot when the abbot was going hunting. The only villein-holding along this street was Rougheys, now Roffey Hall. Roughey probably means Rock-wood, for an early form of the name is Rochey. It was originally a half-virgate, but as in other cases the time came when no villein-tenant could be obtained. The abbot then leased the holding to Ellis Swerder at a yearly rent of 40s for the long term of ninety years, on condition that he built on the site a hall 24 feet by 14 feet, a barn 50 feet by 24 feet, a 'shepenhouse' 16 feet by 10 feet, and a kitchen 16 feet by 12 feet. No doubt there would be a garret in the roof over the hall, and perhaps over the kitchen also, to provide some sleeping accommodation; but the specification of what is evidently regarded as a superior dwelling in the year 1430 suggests the miserable nature of the medieval home, and explains why practically no domestic buildings of pre-Tudor date have survived.

Foster Street, meaning the street of the forester, another link with hunting, runs from Hobbs Cross to the common, which in the old extents is always called Harlow Plain. Along this street were several scattered tenements, including two freeholds, Burrs and Searles and one half-virgate called Wodewardes. Just before reaching the common a road breaks away to the south, leading to the manor of Welds. On the north as soon as the common is reached a lane, called Langley Lane, led to the site of the old villein holding of Andrew le Yerdlyng. This was later known as Old House, but has long since been demolished. The lane continued past Hubbards Hall and the Chantry House to Parnels-bregge and the church. Lying some way back from the common on the north side was the manor of Kitchen Hall, now a modern farm house. On the other side a wide green track, now called Mill Street, led to the Kitchen Hall windmill and linked up with Hastingwood Common. At the lower end of Mill Street stands Shonks, a small farmstead which took its name from a family called Shank. In 1430 John Shank was tried at the abbot's court for making a false complaint.

The common was bounded on the south by Harlow Park. This was the chief wood of the demesne, and when it was enclosed the surrounding woodland was cleared and divided into a series of fields called Parklond. A traveller from Harlow to Waltham and London had a choice of ways: he could either go by Mill Street and Hastingwood past the southern side of Harlow Park, or across the common to the north of the park and up the present London Road. By either route he would reach Rundells, and from there take the road which strikes west past Latton Priory. Potter Street ran from the common north to the present Kingsdon Hall (home of William de Kyngestone, *c.* 1351), which stands on the site of the old homestead of Thomas at-Cross. He took his name from a wayside cross, called Mantel's Cross, which stood at the junction of two diverging roads, one of which led to the market, the other wending its way east and north to the moot-mound and the church. The road leading northwards to (Old) Harlow market was a newly-constructed one following the line of the present London Road for most of the way, but leading into the market probably opposite the 'Crown', i.e. to the west of the present road; it was called New Street and as it was not an ancient thoroughfare dwellings were not built along it. It passed only one old tenement, the villein-holding of Groves, occupied by a family who took their name from the adjoining Latton Grove. The site of Groves is near what is now called 'Maypole Corner'.

Potter Street took its name from the potters who plied their trade there centuries ago. The earliest mention of a Harlow potter is probably the Assize Roll of 1254 where Cok le Pottere de Pottershull is named. Later Harlow court rolls make many references to potters and to Potter Street: a characteristic pottery called Metropolitan Slipware was made in the district. The industry was still flourishing in the seventeenth century, but has long since been abandoned. Before the making of New

Street the regular route to Harlow was by the old Church Way, now an indistinct footpath. This originally led over the lands of New Hall in an almost straight line to the Moot-mound, and continued on past Mulberry Green to Hoo Street. At the Moot-mound another track branched off to the right leading to Harlow church.

Harlow Market comprised the present Market Street, Fore Street and High Street, though none of these names appear in the medieval surveys. The Market-place, called the Market Plain, originally was an open space stretching from the southern side of Fore Street to where St John's church now stands. The space was first narrowed by the building of the dwellings which form the northern side of Market Street; another row of dwellings was erected separating Market Street from Fore Street; this was called 'the middle row' or 'the middle of the market' (*media rengea*). Most of the buildings in the market were shops or small dwellings with stalls in front. In the centre of the market stood the market cross; at the Latton end, just on the boundary of that parish, there was a wayside cross called Latton Cross. The dwellings along the south side of the market backed on to a rough pasture called Mark Hall Moors, later part of Mark Hall park and now East Park. At Latton Cross a lane branched off to the north leading to the meadows; this was called Foreleys Lane. The High Street appears in the surveys as 'the way from the market to the church'. The houses down the High Street were not shops, as now, but the dwellings of small-holders, who had their strips of land in the fields which lay just south of the High Street, and which were called 'Mollond' and 'Chipping Field'. The latter means 'market-field', the former means the land held by the molmen. These were small-holders who paid a money rent for their two or three acres instead of doing manual service. 'Mol' or 'mal' means 'money'; from which the word 'blackmail' is derived. The molmen at Harlow thought themselves superior to the villeins. In 1290 Abbot John de Northwold held an enquiry at the outer gate of his manor of Harlowbury to define the status of the tenants of 'Mollond'. The jury, consisting of the principal inhabitants of the town, found that although Hugh, Samson and other former abbots had relaxed the services due from these tenants and substituted certain rents in money, yet they held nothing by charter, and were taxable in every way like those who did customary service and were altogether of villein status.

The Market (Old Harlow) was always something of a self-contained community separate from the rest of the vill; indeed, as at Epping, Harlow was sometimes divided into the Market and the Upland. Among the Augmentation Office records are some details about the valuation of the St Edmund's property at Harlow at the time of the Dissolution, including this note—'Also to be remembered that the

Abbots of Bury at the first time of their entry have a custom called
Coope-sylver or Palfrey-money to the amount of £4 17s 8d whereof
was gathered of the part of the Market 27s, and of the part of the
Uppeland 70s 8d, as appears in old records'. It was fairly common custom to welcome a new lord at the holding of his first court with a
present called a recognition, which beginning as a voluntary gift in
time became a tax. The tax levied at Harlow on the consecration of each
new abbot was intended to provide him with a silver cup or a riding
horse. The amount raised in the market-quarter, where according to
the extent of 1430 there were fifty-four tenants, looks like a levy of 6d
per head.

The site of the Roman Temple was occupied by a wood called
Stonegrove, belonging to the Abbot of St Edmund; this is shown as a
wood in the Altham map of 1616. In 1308 John Hubert of Harlow came
with two greyhounds and took a doe at 'Stanegraveshelle', and carried
the venison to his house at Harlow; for this he was imprisoned until he
had paid a fine. Adjoining Stonegrove there was a small open field
divided into strips; this was later enclosed. Bromleys and the mill were
the only properties north of the Harlow to Netteswell road, except for
a cottage or two. Medieval Latton Street left the highroad opposite
Bromleys Farm, the first section of it being known as Watery Lane.
The way ran straight to the church of St Mary-at-Latton and passed
along the west and south sides of the churchyard. Opposite the
west end of the church was a lane leading to the vicarage, now
Moot House, which is shown in the Altham estate map as an old
moated house. The map also shows some small erection in the roadway
at the junction of Vicarage Lane; here was the whipping-post, and
probably also the stocks and cage. After passing the south side of the
churchyard, the road straightened out again; at this angle stood the
entrance of Mark Hall; a little further, on the other side of the road, was
the rival manor of Latton Hall. From the church the old road ran
south to Puffers Green, passing on the way the old wooden animal
pound. Puffers Green is a corruption of Purfoots Green. Purfoots on
the east and Cocks on the west were the principal holdings in this part
of the village, though there were several small tenements round the
green. Purfoots, later called Sawpit Cottage and now known as
Coppings, was a small farm adjoining the sawpit. Cocks is now called
Puffers Green Farm. From the green there were two roads to the
common, Latton Street bearing to the left and Brook Lane to the right.
Brook Lane passed two small farmsteads called Brooks and Blocks, and
emerged on Mark Hall Common. Latton Street carried on to Latton
Common, the last section, just before the clap-gate, being known as
'the butts' (possibly a reference to the archery 'meets' which were held

there). Latton Common, attached to Latton Hall, was not extensive; it was bounded on the south by some tenements, which probably represented encroachments on the waste. The fields adjoining the common on either side of the clap-gate are named on the estate-map 'Shypcot Rydden' and 'Clossett Rydden'; these fields were evidently cut out of the common. The former indicates the place where the lord of Latton Hall folded his sheep, the latter means the small enclosure taken out of the waste. Mark Hall Common was very much larger; between the common proper and the great wood of Latton Park was a stretch of land covered with bushes and scrub known as 'the bushes'. From this the common was usually known as Bush Fair Common and the great fair held there was called 'the Bush Fair'.

At Netteswell, apart from the alterations along the river valley, the chief changes were brought about by enclosures and later by the development of the town which completely altered the medieval plan which existed until recently. The road from (Old) Harlow came down Harlow Hill, now a part of the Town Park cycle track system, to Netteswell Cross, where there was a wayside cross called 'Colynes-crouche' or Collins Cross. Crouch or crutch is a common Old English word for a cross; there were two or three other crosses in this area bearing this same name of Collins Cross. The sunken road to Netteswell Cross was called 'Holstrate'—the hollow, or sunken street. At the cross a lane ran north to the mill and meadows. Except for the mill, the only old house in this section is Marshgate Farm, but that does not go back beyond *c.* 1600. The mill was known as Burnt Mill as far back as the reign of Elizabeth I. The sloping field from Edinburgh Way to Harlow Town Station occupied now by Longmans Green & Co's offices, upon which the former Spring Street houses stood, was called Millers Wells, and was full of springs which yielded a good water-supply. Across the way was Tunmanmeade, the townsmen's meadow, where strips were allotted to each holding.

At Netteswell Cross there was a cluster of tenements and these continued up the south side of the Parndon road (now known as Park Lane); on the other side of the road, now part of the Town Park, was a large plough-land called 'Mukemere'. The main street—now School Lane—ran from the cross southwards through the centre of the village area past Netteswellbury and the church of St Andrew to Tye Green Village and the commons.

At Netteswell the chief tenants, the townsmen, were half-virgaters; four of these dwelt at the cross. Their holdings have gone by various names, but most of them can be located. The one occupied in 1235 by Richard the ploughman was later called The Dashes; it was demolished, and Broomhill Cottages, Park Lane, stand on the site. The existing

Cross Farm was originally known as Whitewaits. Hill House retains its old name, and opposite it stands Snows, or Oldhouse Farm, called in the fifteenth century Mangers. From Mangers to Tye Green there were no houses except the Rectory, which has always occupied its site near the junction of Second Avenue and Manston Road, and the manor of Netteswellbury, separated from the Rectory by the moors and the fishponds. Beyond Netteswellbury was another cluster of tenements grouped round Tye Green. These were mostly the homes of small-holders, tilling 6 or 7 acres, but at the lower end of the green on the right was the larger holding already mentioned—Jean's Yerdlyng (i.e. John's Virgate). Fountains Farm is a corruption of Fortunes, a name which applied to a field adjoining the green.

The lower end of the green, before the enclosures, joined on to Copshall Common, which opened out further south on to Netteswell Common. Copshall in 1270 was spelt Copeshelle, and no doubt took its name from a domed hill opposite the entrance to Goldings. Goldings is a modern corruption of Goldsmith, the holdings known in 1465 as 'Goldsmiths anciently called Yorkes' from the family of Richard York *c.* 1270. It was the largest holding in the village and comprised half a hide (60 acres).

Just to the north-west of Goldings lies a small farm for centuries known as Hawkins, but the name was later changed to Crawleys. A family bearing the Danish name of Hacun held a half-virgate here all through the thirteenth and fourteenth centuries. In 1271 there was a wedding-party at the house of John Hacun. Roger Prichard and Gilbert de Westwode were present, and there was a fierce quarrel between them, followed by a free fight, in which Roger struck Gilbert with a mug so that he died instantly.

The road passed Tye Green and reached the Common, where another group of smallholders had their homes. Near the Latton boundary a green lane led to the site of a demolished farm which used to be known as Laylands or Warley Hook; William de Warley held land there in 1235. By an enclosure act of the year 1851 all the open spaces in Netteswell were enclosed including the common field, Tye Green, Copshall Common and Netteswell Common. Part of Nettes-well Common had been enclosed many centuries earlier when the assart was made on Rye Hill, later known as Wood Ridden or the Riddens (Riddings), and a large section between Netteswell Common, Copshall Common, and the main road was fenced in and called Stock Ridden.

The slopes of Rye Hill above Netteswell Common must once have been covered with bracken, for early in the fourteenth century this portion was called Fern Hill; the two cottages below Dorringtons farm are still called Fern Hill Cottages.

At Parndon also the medieval lay-out had been altered by the enclosing of the commons. Great Parndon Common was reached from Netteswell Common by the road, now known as Commonside and Kingsmoor Roads, which passed Stewards and Maunds and descended in a curving slope to the brook. The common lay in the hollow between Parndon woods and the rising ground upon which stand Sumners Farm and Kingsmoor House; it was skirted on the north by the road leading to Richmonds and Jack's Hatch, and linked up with Broadley Common and Nazeing Common. The original manor-house of Parndon, (Jerounds, the home of the Whitsands), lay near the church of St Mary. The principal nucleus at Parndon lay round the crossroads at what is now called Cock Green, then known as Parndon Green. Here roads led east to the common, west to Catherines and the church, south by Water Lane to Tylers Cross and Broadley Common and north by a sharp bend to the ford and Hare Street. A more direct road from Hare Street and the ford passed Linford End and then went by Passmores to Rye Hill Common. Rye Hill Common was attached to the manor of Little Parndon; the greater part of the common was enclosed, and became the home pasture for Dorringtons Farm.

Adjacent to the site of the manor-house at Little Parndon a fine old mill and mill house, relics of a by-gone trade, still stand by Little Parndon lock from which an old lane, called Cats Lane, leads through a ford to Eastwick. Before Parndon Hall park was enclosed there were a few scattered tenements along the road leading up to 'The Elm'. This well-known landmark, a large elm tree, stands at Wych Elm which now occupies the site of the junction of the roads to Netteswell, Hare Street, and Little Parndon. Here there once stood a wayside cross called Stone Cross; in the sixteenth century an adjoining field was called 'Stonecross Field'. The road-plan of the ways to Hare Street, Roydon, and Netteswell remained unchanged from the Middle Ages until the new town development, but the whole character of this part of Little Parndon was altered by the building of the Upper House with its walled garden, stabling and park. This house was erected in the eighteenth century, but was pulled down in 1835.

Chapter 7
The Reformation and the Dissolution of the Monasteries

The middle years of the fifteenth century were much disturbed by civil war. The Wars of the Roses brought all progress to a standstill and checked the natural growth and development which the earlier years of the century had witnessed. The peaceful policy and strong government of the first Tudor king, Henry VII, was maintained by his son, Henry VIII, but this reign was to witness sensational events, which were to be felt throughout the land and changed the whole course of the nation's history through the Reformation and its sequel—the dissolution of the monasteries. Henry was a man of considerable learning and breadth of mind but he was covetous, mean, suspicious and ungrateful, the latter trait summed up so well by Sir Walter Raleigh, 'to many gave he abundant flowers from whence to gather honey and in the end of harvest burnt them in the hive', a reference to the treatment of several of his advisers.

His desire for a son and his infatuation for Anne Boleyn urged him to seek a divorce from Katherine of Aragon. First mooted in 1514 and again in 1528, it was refused by the Pope who did not wish to offend the Emperor Charles, who was Katherine's nephew. Finally, a way out of this impasse was suggested by a young Cambridge tutor, Thomas Cranmer.

Many of the characters of this drama had some link with this district. Henry was at that time negotiating for the manor of Netteswellbury. Temple Roydon was granted to Anne Boleyn as part of her dowry. Thomas Cromwell, Henry's chief minister, had designs on Harlowbury as described in Chapter 5, while one of his chief opponents, the martyr, Sir Thomas More, married Jane, daughter of John Colt, lord of Nether Hall (Roydon), Little Parndon and Welds, and at Waltham, Cranmer found the formula which severed the English church from Rome. Mary Tudor, unpleasantly remembered as 'Bloody Mary' because of the religious persecutions which occurred during her reign, used Hunsdon House as one of her principal places of residence before coming to the throne and was there when Edward VI died.

Long before the Act of 1534 by which Henry became head of the church there was in the country and in Essex in particular opposition to Romanist worship. The Lollards and the circulation of the Bible forged a movement supported by people of varying degrees of Protestant belief. One of the first to sign this Act when it came before the Lower House of Convocation in 1534 was the Abbot of Waltham, followed later by signed declarations of fourteen priests of the deanery of Harlow.

The effects of the Reformation were gradual, for Henry and a great many of his advisers and supporters were conservatives in religion and they ensured that the forms of service to which they had been used were not changed.

The evils of the perpetual and absentee rectors, and plurality of livings, continued to exist within the church after the Reformation and the churches within this town were no exception. In 1350 Richard Drax was rector of Harlow, but held in addition a canonry at Howden, and a canonry of Chichester with the prebend of Colworth. Much of his time was spent in attempting to obtain from the Pope further emoluments. In 1354 he applied for the canonry and prebend of St Patrick's, Dublin, and in 1359 obtained the archdeaconery of Totnes. During his period as rector of Harlow he appears to have lived at Avignon and it is doubtful if he ever set foot within the church, possibly paying a vicar or chaplain to serve the cure. After the Reformation in 1564 Richard Harrison was appointed rector of Harlow by Queen Elizabeth I; he was also rector of Beaumont (1566–86), vicar of Bradfield (1569–77), marrying Anne Ingold at Netteswell in 1564, an act that would have deprived him of his livings under Henry and Mary.

The same position appears in Netteswell where Thomas Wilkinson (1524–31) served the cure; he was also rector of Stanway from 1514 to 1531.

Frequently the fabric of the church suffered, the absentee rectors being only concerned with the emoluments, leaving the state of the church to providence. At Harlow in 1520 Sir Edwin Whytstone, chaplain of the perpetual chantry of St Petronilla, was licensed to be absent for one year on account of the ruinous state of the chantry.

The dissolution of the monasteries which followed the Act of Supremacy was a continuation of a policy which had its roots in the fifteenth century, when random suppressions had taken place. Under Cardinal Wolsey this had given place to a systematic policy of suppression.

Monasticism had lost its glamour, for the religious fervour of the benefactors had turned into other channels: chantries, hospitals and educational institutions. In the towns which had arisen around the great abbeys riots had frequently taken place; nevertheless, it is doubtful if the monks were worse landlords than the laity. Probably much of the disillusionment with the religious arose from their worldliness. When the Augustinian priory of Burley in Suffolk was suppressed in 1538 its inmates numbered eighty-four, consisting of canons, carters, shepherds, woodkeepers, dairymaids, laundry women, huntsmen, barbers, waiters and other servants, with the local gentry often holding high office within the religious houses and frequently interfering with the internal administration.

In 1535 Henry VIII instituted an enquiry into the monasteries, which required that the wealth, numbers and revenue be made known to the King's commissioners. The results of this enquiry are embodied in a vast collection known as the Valor Ecclesiasticus which provided Henry with a very accurate assessment of the state of the religious houses; by 1540 this had all passed into his hands. Such was the magnitude of the lands, goods and wealth that a special department was set up to administer the disposal of the property and to pay pensions to the dispossessed monks, most of whom did not seem to object to the dissolution of their houses. One of the results was the rise of a new class of landed gentry, for a great many rectories fell into lay hands.

In the parish of Harlow the principal manor of Harlowbury, as we have seen, was purchased by Lady Addington and her son Thomas; they also bought the rectory which carried with it the advowson of the vicarage. The Addington family held this manor and presented the vicars until between 1670 and 1680. It is doubtful whether the Addingtons ever made their home at Harlow. In 1621 Richard Hanchet was their tenant there and in 1659, shortly before they severed their connection with the town, Harlowbury was leased to John Cass. The present house dates from this period. Richard Addington left the manor by his will to Arthur Champernowne and Richard Way. On January 24, 1680, the beneficiaries leased the property for one year at a nominal rent (five shillings, and one peppercorn if demanded) to Sir Francis North, Chief Justice of the Common Pleas and created 1st Baron Guilford in 1683. This lease was quickly followed by the sale of the manor by the same people to Sir Francis North for £8,300. On December 13, 1681, Sir Francis leased the manor to his brother Roger, and the following day Roger underleased the property back to Sir Francis. The reasons for this transaction can only be a matter of speculation.

Latton Priory was not dissolved; it came to a natural end for want of brethren to serve it, just before the smaller houses were suppressed, the last prior, John Taylor, deserting it. Whether or not he entered another house of his order or became a secular clergyman is not known. The annual income of this house amounted to £12 (about £480 today) an extremely small sum, with the possible additional payment of the vicar's fees of Latton to one of the canons. In about 1538 it was granted to Sir Henry Parker, KB, Lord Morley of Great Hallingbury, who had already obtained possession of Mark Hall, but in 1562 James Altham acquired from Lord Morley both Mark Hall and the priory and the Altham family retained these two properties until late in the eighteenth century. They also held the rectory and the advowson of the vicarage of Latton.

At Netteswell the last Abbot of Waltham, Robert Fuller, was allowed to retain the manor of Netteswellbury and the advowson of the rectory for the rest of his life. It will be remembered that Henry VIII had been planning to secure this manor as part of a great estate which he was contemplating on either side of the Stort, and for which he had already obtained Hunsdon House and Temple Roydon, but with the fall of Anne Boleyn, for whom this estate was intended, he changed his mind, and Netteswell remained the property of Waltham Abbey until the dissolution. Fuller only survived for two years, when the estate was purchased by Richard Heigham. In 1560 John Heigham sold it to Richard Weston of Skreens Park, near Writtle. A family named Finch were tenants of this manor before the Dissolution and continued to farm it under the Heighams and the Westons.

Waltham Abbey's other possession in this town, the manor of Catherines at Great Parndon, together with a third of the advowson of the rectory, was also purchased by Richard Heigham.

In 1180 the canons had left Parndon Abbey ('Canons') for a more favoured site granted to them at Beeleigh near Maldon. After the dissolution of Beeleigh Abbey the manor of Canons was granted to Sir Thomas Darcy, and was sold by him to John Hanchet. Hanchet's daughter Martha married Edward Turnor and brought him this estate. In 1602 the Turnors alienated this manor to Edward Altham of Mark Hall. Sir Edward Altham died possessed of it in 1632, and his widow Joan still held it in 1645, when she was presented at Quarter Sessions for not maintaining Canons' Bridge. From the Althams this manor passed to the Farmers; Sir Edward Farmer made his home here, and under him the house was considerably enlarged.

Of the manors which had not been held by the monasteries the majority came into the hands of two families already mentioned—the families of Bugge and Colt. At the time of the Reformation the Bugges owned Moor Hall, Kitchen Hall and New Hall and these they held for about two centuries. Their name appears on almost every document dealing with Old Harlow, and they seem to have been trustees for most of the charities. Their name occasionally appears on the Quarter Sessions rolls, as when, in 1580, John Bugge was presented along with Richard Shelley, butcher, John Gladwyn, yeoman, Thomas Stace, butcher, Nicholas Sybley, mercer, and John Brown, shoemaker, for playing bowls on Christmas Day in a place called Pepper Alley in Harlow, contrary to the statute. This was probably the statute passed

some forty years earlier to discourage all sport except archery. There
are brasses in St Mary and St Hugh's church to Edward Bugge who
died in 1582, and to his son Richard who died in 1636.

The Colts came a little later than the Bugges. Thomas Colt had
purchased the manor of Nether Hall, Roydon, about the year 1450, and
built the fortified manor-house there, now a picturesque ruin. His son
John Colt acquired the manors of Little Parndon and Welds in Harlow.
He died in 1521 and was followed by his eldest son Sir George Colt.
The family gradually dwindled in importance, and became more closely
associated with Suffolk, but continued to hold these three manors until
well into the seventeenth century.

The two portions of the manor of Great Parndon, Jerounds and
Stewards, which were not held by Waltham Abbey, after passing
through various hands came into the crown and were granted by
Edward VI to the City of London, and applied by the corporation to
their charitable foundations. They were assigned, together with one
third of the advowson of the rectory, to St Thomas's Hospital. The
wood in Parndon known as Hospital Wood takes its name from this
source. The other third of the advowson seems to have been sold away
from the land before it came into the crown. At a later date the hospital
also acquired the manor of Catherines, so that the three portions of the
manor of Great Parndon were once more united.

The Charter or Letters Patent by which Edward VI granted these
lands to the City of London for their charitable foundations (and in
particular, St Thomas's Hospital) contains this following preamble:

'AFTER RECITING that His Majesty pitying the miserable estate
of the Poor fatherless decrepit aged sick infirm and impotent persons
languishing under various kinds of diseases And also of his special
grace thoroughly considering the honest pious endeavours of his
most humble and obedient subjects the Mayor & Commonalty &
Citizens of the City of London who by all ways and means diligently
studied for the good provision of the Poor and of every sort of them
And that by such reason and care neither children yet being in their
infancy should lack good education and instruction nor when they
should obtain riper years be destitute of honest callings and occu-
pations whereby they might honestly exercise themselves in some
good faculty and service for the advantage and utility of the
Commonwealth nor that the sick or diseased when they should be
recovered and restored to health might remain idle and lazy vagabonds of the State but that they in like manner might be placed and
compelled to labour and honest and wholesome employments . . .'

The reference to 'idle and lazy vagabonds' relates to the growing problem which led to the early Elizabethan Poor Law.

The manor of Hubbard's Hall continued to be held by the descendants of Sir John Shaa, Lord Mayor of London until the end of the reign of Elizabeth when it came into the possession of the Reeves. This family held the manor for several generations, their name being perpetuated by the almshouses on the Sheering Road, founded under the will of Francis Reeve, who died in 1639. It was this same Francis Reeve who was presented at Quarter Sessions in the reign of Charles I for setting up a mill—probably a horse-mill—in the highway from Foster Street to Harlow church and enclosing the way. The highway mentioned is the old church way which led from the west end of Foster Street, where it opens on to the common, by Langley Lane past Old House, Hubbard's Hall and the Chantry, to Parnelsbridge and Churchgate Street.

The effects of the Dissolution were felt not so much in the transference of ownership, as in the sudden cessation of the services which the monks had rendered to society. They had cared for the wayfarer and ministered to the needy. Medieval hospitals were all monastic foundations. There had been many of these not only in the towns, but dotted about the countryside; the majority of them were swept away with the monasteries, and no new institutions took their place. Many of the greater monasteries had cultivated the fine arts and they had been an important factor in the education of the upper classes. The dissolution of the religious houses was followed in the reign of Edward VI by the suppression of the chantries and the forfeiture of all the bequests which pious churchmen had made for the salvation of their souls.

The changes in worship resulting from the Reformation did not take place suddenly. The same priests conducted the same services at the same hours, sometimes in Latin, sometimes in English. The words in either tongue were probably unintelligible to the villager, who for so long had been used to 'the blessed mutter of the Mass'. But he understood its form and it fulfilled his spiritual needs. The introduction of the English Bible and later the English Prayer Book must of necessity have been slow. The only visible changes in the church were the removal of rood screens and images, the destruction of altars and the introduction of communion tables. Of the priests who held benefices in Harlow prior to the Reformation all continued in office.

In 1547 Parliament passed an act for the suppression of the chantries, the intention of the act being that the proceeds from the sale of the chantries should be set aside for the relief of the poor, the founding of grammar schools and the extension of universities. Little of the money was used for these high ideals, most of it being used in the building of fortifications and the levying of soldiers.

In 1559–60, Elizabeth I instituted an enquiry into the state of the churches in the realm, which she had found to be in a state of disarray. Over a third of the bishoprics were vacant, hundreds of parishes lacked clergy, and many churches were in a ruinous condition. The Bishop of London's visitation for this enquiry gives some brief comments on the state of the clergy in the parishes now in the town. Roger Byrcheleye at Little Parndon and Edward Hayles at Netteswell were 'not resydente and there was noo hospitalitie kept, not able to preach'. At Latton, William fflecther is 'resydente and keepeth hospitalitie, not able to preach', whilst much the same is said of William Howe of Harlow. At Great Parndon, Charles Parker is recorded as being absent and thought to be at a University 'beyonde the sea'. His 'farmour keapeth hospitalitie and one Michil Carhil, priest, serveth the cure'. Charles Parker had refused to conform to the articles of 1571, was deprived of his benefice and had probably fled to the Continent.

These attacks on the church represented by the dissolution of religious houses and chantries also led to a cooling of the devotion hitherto shown by the laity towards their parish churches, and in the reign of Elizabeth I churchgoing had to be enforced by law. The Quarter Sessions rolls of the reigns of Elizabeth I and James I note several presentments for neglecting to attend church. Thus, in 1603, it was reported of Roger Ward, clerk, that 'he hath come to us in the parish of Harlow and hath been with us a certain time before Christmas until the ninth of January, and hath not observed the Book of Common Prayer, moreover, he doth neither say the Creed, nor the Ten Commandments, nor the Epistle nor Gospel'. At the same time Robert Hiles of Netteswell was presented in that 'he is excommunicated and hath not come to our church, not this whole year'.

The religious changes caused little disturbance to the clergy, and the continuity between pre-reformation days and the first Elizabethan age was unbroken. There were, however, great changes in clerical personnel. Before the Reformation, besides the incumbent there had been numerous assistants, chantry-chaplains, parish-priests, vicar's chaplains and the like. The incumbents had for the most part been unmarried, with few ties, and therefore were much more mobile; exchanges of livings had been very frequent, and incumbencies seldom lasted for more than a few years. Now the chantries had been swept away, and the numerous chaplains attached to the churches disappeared. The clergy were now for the most part married and less inclined to move. Several of them were pluralists, and in such cases their additional livings were entrusted to curates, a term which only came into use in the Tudor period, signifying not as now an assistant-priest but a clergyman in temporary charge of a parish.

The suppression of the chantries and the disbanding of the assistant clergy resulted in more church property passing into lay ownership. The old vicarage at the corner of Churchgate Street was sold, and Meadham was built on the site. The priest's house in Churchgate Street, on the south side of the churchyard, was also disposed of, while the chantry-priest's house was in 1549 granted to Thomas Marsh. This house stood at the east end of the churchyard, on a site now occupied by the Newman Almshouses. The Chantry House came into the Crown and was leased by Elizabeth I to several different parties and was finally granted by James I to Michael Cole and John Rowdon. In 1615 it was purchased by Alexander Stafford, who built the present house and whose tomb stands in the south transept of the church, where the chantry was originally founded.

Whether or not the change of ownership from monastic to lay affected the tenants of manorial property generally is debatable, but it appears that in Harlow some attempt was made by the Addingtons to alter the position of the copyholders. John Gladwyn (d. 1617) who held lands from the manor of Harlowbury by copyhold, spent many years fighting in the law courts on behalf of the copyholders. It cost him considerable time and money to achieve justice; he also accused the trustees of mis-applying some charitable funds. The lord of the manor cannot have grieved much on his death. Such was the respect of the copyholders for John Gladwyn that when his brass in Harlow church was mounted on the north transept wall after the fire of 1708 they provided a new slab so that it could be replaced in its old position in the floor. Today it is back on the north transept wall.

For the ordinary man and woman the change was simply a matter of new landlords, often greedier than the monks, a slow change in church services and spoliation of the interior decoration. With the regime introduced by Mary Tudor, persecutions of Protestants once again became part of the religious turmoil. Under her regime, priests who had married were deprived of their livings or hurriedly put their wives aside. Those people who openly resisted the Marian institutions in religion often died at the stake and Mary's marriage to Philip of Spain finally lost her the popular support of the people. Later under Elizabeth I many of the Roman Catholic faith were to die at the stake and as a result many Catholics fled the country.

Chapter 8
The Stuarts and their struggle with Parliament

The reign of James I opened unpropitiously for the people of Essex. Towards the end of the year 1603 there was a severe outbreak of the plague, which had occurred periodically ever since the black year of 1349. This district does not seem to have suffered as badly as some parts of the county judging from the church registers, but these are not always a reliable guide at abnormal periods. The Latton register states that 'George Warde was buried the eighteenth of December, who died of the plague', and three similar entries follow. In the register of St Mary's church, Great Parndon, the burial entries for 1603 have evidently been inserted some time after the actual ceremonies, owing to a vacancy in the benefice, and probably the record is incomplete; it reads as follows:

'John Roberts was buried the eleventh of December.
Elizabeth, wife of Richard Pickbone, same day.
About which time was buried one John—, an
 Aqua vitae man, that died at Edward Adams' house.
And a little before Pickbones' wife was Mother
 Underwood buried.
Anne Kenrick was buried on December 30.
Richard Leech, parson of Paringdon, about Maytide.
Thomas, son of Nicholas Abbots, on January 12.
William, son of Edward Adams, about Shrovetide,
 which was the 19th of February.
Samuel, son of George Randal, buried on August 15, 1603'

James had hardly ascended the throne before he received petitions from the two extreme religious sections, for both the Roman Catholics and the Puritans had hoped that he would favour their cause. But James had determined to pursue the middle course adopted by Elizabeth. He might have been prepared to relax some of the restrictions imposed on the Roman Catholics, but realizing that Parliament was sternly opposed to any such course he did nothing to adjust their grievances. The Puritans presented a petition, signed by many Essex ministers, seeking further reforms. The King had even less sympathy with their demands than with the Roman Catholics, but in order to examine them he summoned a conference at Hampton Court in 1604. The outcome of the conference was a confirmation of the existing regulations. A new prayer-book was issued with very slight alterations; a new English

version of the Bible was authorized; and a committee was appointed
to revise the church's canons. The first reaction to the Hampton Court
Conference came from a small coterie of Roman Catholic fanatics, who
despairing of any help from either King or Parliament determined to
overthrow both. Soon after, in 1605, came the Gunpowder Plot,
exposed through an anonymous letter sent to Lord Morley and
Monteagle, great-grandson of the Lord Morley who sold Mark Hall
to the Althams. Whether this was a plot by the Catholics to destroy
King and Parliament, or whether it was a plot by Robert Cecil, Earl of
Salisbury and Chief Minister to King James I, to discredit the Catholics,
it brought them all under suspicion and facilitated the passage through
Parliament of the anti-Catholic legislation of 1606.

Many leading men in Parliament were Puritans, and the King's lack
of sympathy with the extreme Protestants resulted in increasing opposition from the Commons, and laid the foundations for the bitter dis-
sensions of the next reign. The Puritans received another rebuff when
the King published his Declaration about Sports, encouraging certain
recreations and pursuits on Sunday. The King's conservative policy and
the promulgation of the canons did much to stabilize religion, and some
attempt was made to restore order, to improve the condition of the
churches, and to bring back some dignity of worship. At St Andrew's,
Netteswell the church was evidently refurnished and a new pulpit and
reading-desk installed; little of this work has survived later restorations,
but part of the Jacobean pulpit still stands, bearing the date 1618. The
medieval altars had all been removed, and communion-tables set up in
their place; at St Mary's church, Little Parndon, the Jacobean table
in the vestry once served this purpose. The Puritan reformers objected
to these tables being placed altar-wise against the east wall, and in many
cases they had been brought out of the sanctuary and set up in the body
of the church.

Through some lapse the patronage of Great Parndon seems to have
reverted to the crown just as James came to the throne. In the summer
of 1603 he presented to that rectory Dr Roger Dod, who was also vicar
of Epping and archdeacon of Shrewsbury. The author of the 'State of
the Clargie in Essex', who has seldom anything good to say, described
Dod as a pluralist but an able preacher. He later became Bishop of
Meath. Dod held the rectory of Great Parndon for little more than a
year, when he was succeeded by Valentine Carey, another pluralist,
who became Dean of St Paul's in 1614 and Bishop of Exeter in 1621.

With Parliament leaning so strongly towards Puritanism and gravely
disapproving of King James's extravagance and his court favourites, it
was obvious that his successor would have to tread with caution.
Instead, Charles began his reign by contracting a marriage with a

Roman Catholic princess, Henrietta, daughter of the King of France, at a time when Rome was both feared and suspected, and at the same time pledged his word that he would remove the disabilities imposed upon Roman Catholics, a pledge which Parliament absolutely refused to implement.

From the very outset Charles and his Parliament were hopelessly at cross purposes, and the King was unfortunate in his choice of advisers. The minister who had the largest share of Charles's confidence and the greatest influence on the conduct of affairs was Sir Richard Weston, a lawyer and a diplomat, who had become Chancellor of the Exchequer under James I. Weston, like his father and grandfather before him, was lord of the manor of Netteswell, though he made his home at Skreens Park. Towards the end of his life he was associated more closely with Hampshire, becoming governor of the Isle of Wight and taking up his residence at Carisbrooke Castle. In 1628 he became Lord High Treasurer, and in 1634 was created Earl of Portland, but died in the following year. He lies buried in one of the eastern chapels of Winchester Cathedral, where his effigy magnificently wrought in bronze rests on a large altar tomb. Weston was not popular, and was suspected of a leaning towards Romanism, but he was anxious to maintain peace at all costs and pursued a cautious policy; his death at a critical time in Charles's career was something of a disaster.

Before his elevation to the peerage Weston had parted with the manor of Netteswell, having sold it to Sir William Martin of Woodford, who had been sheriff of Essex in 1631. Three generations of Martins made their home at Netteswellbury; under them the house was rebuilt and became a pleasant country-seat. The Martins were the first lords of the manor since the Conquest to reside at Netteswell. When the family died out in the middle of the eighteenth century the estate was purchased by Thomas Blackmore of Briggens in Hunsdon, and eventually the manor-house was pulled down and a farmhouse built in its place. Little remains of the home of the Martins beyond the walled garden on the south bank of the pond at Second Avenue and some panelling which was taken out of the old house, and is now on the east wall of St Andrew's church, Netteswell, on both sides of the altar. Cuthbert Martin, son and heir of Sir William, was sheriff in 1654, during his father's lifetime; his name occurs as a local magistrate. Cuthbert was succeeded by his son William, who died childless.

After King Charles had dispensed with Parliament, he was forced to seek some new sources of revenue. His first scheme was to revive ancient claims to forest land, and to attempt to include within the forest pale wide stretches of country which had been disafforested ever since the boundaries were fixed in the reign of Edward I. Many landlords

paid large sums of money to keep their estates outside the forest; among
them was Sir William Martin who had recently purchased Netteswellbury, and who under protest paid £500 to free his land. Not un-
naturally we find Sir William a few years later supporting the Parliament against the King.

James Altham of Mark Hall received a similar demand, but there is
no evidence to show whether the demand was met. The forest claim
proved an insufficient and unsatisfactory method of filling the royal
coffers and was alienating the class from whom the King might expect
his chief support, so that it was soon dropped, and the King based his
hopes of raising revenue on the ship-money. James Altham, in spite of
his anxiety about the demands on his estate, remained a Royalist, and
when the civil war broke out joined the forces of the King. We have
more intimate knowledge of the Althams than of any other family in our
area, for much family correspondence has survived. The Althams
occupied Mark Hall for well over two centuries, and as they also
acquired Latton Priory and Latton Hall, they owned the whole of
Latton and a small section of (Old) Harlow.

James Altham, an ironmonger, who had been sheriff of London in
1557, and had purchased Mark Hall in 1562, was sheriff of Essex in
1570. His eldest son Thomas was a Roman Catholic, and for some time
led a fugitive existence in the West Country, and in Wales. One of
Thomas's daughters became a nun at Bruges. Disinherited by his
father, Thomas never returned to Mark Hall. Edward, the second son,
inherited Mark Hall, where he died in 1605. His eldest son, Sir James,
married Elizabeth Barrington of Barrington Hall, Hatfield Broad Oak.
The Barringtons were connected by marriage with the Cromwells,
and were strong Parliamentarians. Sir James Altham's only child, Joan,
married Oliver St John, a Parliamentary leader, and later Solicitor-
general in Cromwell's Parliament. Sir James only held Mark Hall for
five years, dying in 1610, when his brother Sir Edward Altham
succeeded to the estate. Sir Edward's second wife was Joan Leventhorpe of Shingle Hall, Sawbridgeworth; and it is from her correspondence that we are able to follow the fortunes of her numerous
family, and get occasional glimpses of life at Mark Hall.

Lady Altham's eldest son James was the soldier who fought for his
King. John was a barrister with chambers at Gray's Inn. Leventhorpe
was a wine-merchant; he was the business man of the family, and
eventually followed his eldest brother at Mark Hall. Edward was
religiously minded; he later became a Roman Catholic and settled
abroad, where he is said to have been admitted into a religious community. Emmanuel was the rolling stone, an adventurer, always in need
of money; after the Restoration he obtained a commission in the King's

guard. Sir Edward Altham died in 1632; some years later, in 1640, his widow set up a monument to the Altham family. This monument is mentioned in the account of a disgraceful incident which happened that year. King Charles had translated William Laud from the bishopric at Bath to London in 1628 and the new bishop was much concerned at the irreverence and low standard of worship in his diocese. Later, when he became Archbishop of Canterbury, he issued instructions to the clergy and wardens of all churches ordering them to replace the communion-table within the sanctuary and surround it with railings to prevent profanation. The Laudian reforms, coming at a time when the Puritans were urgently petitioning against much milder regulations, excited high feeling; occasionally, as at Latton, they led to ill-advised demonstrations. In one of the Quarter Sessions Bundles there is a series of statements made before a magistrate of an incident which took place in St Mary-at-Latton church on January 1, 1641. Morning prayers had just been said and some men were ringing the bells, when two of them went down into the body of the church to look at the new Altham monument. Whether or not there had been some argument about the changes in the sanctuary is uncertain, but suddenly one of the men started pulling down the altar rails. The railings were carried out of the church, thrown over the fence, hacked to pieces with an axe, and then set on fire. Several men lent a hand, and, after they had destroyed the railings, pulled the table out and restored it to its old position in the body of the church, they sent for ale which they drank in the porch and afterwards in the belfry. Information to this effect was laid by John Starkeys, servant to Mr Denne, the vicar, and by John Case, servant to James Altham, Esq. As a result four of the offenders were examined by Edward Palmer of Nazeing, a magistrate, when one of them, William Skynner, made the following statement:

'The sayde William Skynner sayeth, that on Friday, the first daye of this present Januarie, hee this examinat, after morning prayer in the parish church of Latton aforesayde, did together with Jeremye Reeve of Latton, and the persons above named and sundrye others of the sayde parishe goe to ringing in the sayde church. And sayeth that hee and Reeve, after the sayde ringing, did repaire first into the Chancell of that church to looke upon Sir Edward Altham's monument there standing, where this examinat sayeth that Reeve first moved this examinat to pull downe the rales from about the Communion table together with him the sayde Reeve, which hee this examinat together with Reeve, who first began the same, accordingly did. But this examinat denyeth that hee, or Reeve, or anye other person did use an axe or hatchet or other instrument about it, but pulled the same downe with their hands onelye. And further sayeth that whiles they were pulling down the sayde rales and before they were all pulled downe the sayde Wennell and Vinton came to them and pulled downe part thereof, and helped together with Reeve and this examinat to carrye the sayde broken rales out of the church into the churchyard, and to cast them over the churchyard wall into the highe waye, and to sett them on fire neare to the whipping-post. And further sayeth that Reeve did cut and rend the rales so cast into the highe waye, this examinat and the other sayde persons (Wright onelye excepted) beeing then in companye and present; but none of them but Reeve did handle the axe. And hee further sayeth that hee this examinat with the sayde above-named persons and others did laye their moneyes together to the summe of two shillings, and sent Wennell for beere. And the sayde Wennell brought a kilderkin, or such like vessel, of beere for the sayde moneye from the Black Lyon[1] an alehouse in Harlowe, on his shoulders, and sett it downe near the highe waye where the rales were fired. And hee the sayde Skynner further sayeth that the sayde vessel was carryed thence (but hee knoweth not by whome) into the sayde church porch, where the greater part of the sayde beere was dranke by them, the other examinats, and divers others. And sayeth that Henrye Vinton above sayde, did carrye it into the church and into the belfrye, where the remainder was dranke up by themselves and the ringers. And hee lastly sayeth that the reason of his so pulling downe the rales was because they gave offence to his conscience and that the placing of them was against God's lawes and the King's, as appeareth by the twentyeth chapter of Exodus and about the twentyeth verse; and lastly because the rales had been pulled downe in other places without punishment therefore. And this examinat lastly sayeth that hee and the sayde other persons had no weapons at all or any offensive matter about them, and is very sorye for his sayde offence, and confesseth that it was most inadvisedlye done. And this examinat doth not knowe of anye other persons counselling, countenancing, or assisting thereunto.'

During the next three years the breach between King and Parliament widened. London and the eastern counties were wholeheartedly for the Parliament, and the court was transferred to Oxford. The demands of the Puritans for religious reform became more and more insistent and to meet these a Council of Divines was appointed. This council was composed of both clergy and laity; two prominent members came from this neighbourhood, Sir William Cecil, Earl of Salisbury, lord of the manor of Roydon, and Sir Thomas Barrington of Hatfield Broad Oak. The recommendations of the council included drastic limitation of the powers of the bishops, the reconstitution of the church on a presby-

[1] See page 96

terian basis, and the authorization of the Directory in place of the
Prayer-book.

By 1646 a scheme had been drawn up by which each county was
divided into a series of districts, or classes, containing a dozen or more
parishes, while each parish was entrusted to a minister and two or more
deacons. Where the incumbent was prepared to conform to the new
orders, he was left undisturbed; if he refused to do so the benefice was
sequestrated and a new minister placed in charge. There was only one
sequestration in our district; this was at Great Parndon in 1643, where
the Royalist rector, William Osbalston, was deprived of his living. The
following reasons are given for his sequestration:

'For that he in his absence supplied his cure by scandalous and
insufficient curates, and hath in his sermons preached against frequent
preaching affirming it to be properly no service of God, and that it was
never a merry world since there was so much of it, and that if he could
preach twice a day he would not, and that once hearing of common
prayer is better than ten sermons; and hath read in his church the Book
of Sports on the Lord's Day, and encouraged men to football and other
like sports on that day; and hath taught his people that the water in
Baptism doth wash away original sin, and being desired to pray for a
sick child that was two years old said in his prayer that actual sin it had
committed none, and as for original it was washed away at Baptism;
and hath pressed his parishioners to come up to the rails to receive the
Sacrament, professing that otherwise he would not deliver it to them;
and hath threatened to present such of his parishioners as went to
hear sermons elsewhere when they had none at home, calling them
hypocrites and of the tribe of Gad; and said to one of his parishioners
that he could not abide him because he stank of two sermons a day.
And being demanded to contribute to the Association of the Counties
for the Public Defence, said he would first have his throat cut.'
Osbalston was ejected from Great Parndon, and Jeremiah Dike was
appointed in his place.

At Netteswell, Sir William Martin and John Bannister, the two
leading parishioners, appear in the records as deacons; this did not
apparently deter Bannister from laying down a brass to his own memory. In the other parishes the deacons were mostly yeomen or tradesmen, though Robert Reeve, lord of Hubbard's Hall, was one of the
four deacons at the parish church of Harlow (St Mary and St Hugh).

Churches were visited to undo the improvements made by the
Laudian regulations, and to remove anything that might savour of
superstition. Lady Altham in one of her letters mentions such a visit
at St Mary-at-Latton, when the cross was removed from the steeple
and the sanctus-belfry pulled down. The sanctus-bell probably hung in

a little cote at the head of the rood-screen stairway in the south wall of the church. How far the services of the church were altered and the ceremonies discontinued it is difficult to ascertain, and no doubt largely depended on the views and the courage of the minister. Great emphasis was laid upon preaching and it was on their ability as preachers that the clergy were assessed. Thus, Edward Spranger, vicar of Harlow (St Mary and St Hugh) is described as 'an able godly preaching minister', Thomas Denne of St Mary-at-Latton as 'an able and godly preacher', Thomas Cramphorne of St Andrew's Netteswell as 'a godly preaching minister', William Haughton of St Mary's Little Parndon as 'an able preaching minister'. Of Brockett Smith, vicar of Roydon, the report is not so good; of him it is stated 'he preacheth constantly, but is returned to the jurors to be of scandalous life, yet he hath produced good testimonials'.

From 1644 to 1660, when Parliament was supreme and Puritanism in the ascendant, church registers were largely neglected, and throw little light on current events. At St Andrew's church, Netteswell, all through this period Mr Cramphorne failed to enter up his register, though a few entries were inserted, evidently after the Restoration. At St Mary-at-Latton church, Mr Denne continued to keep his register much as before; the number of marriages is well up to the average, and the publication of banns is noted. At St Mary's church, Great Parndon, there are no contemporary entries for this period, but a few have been inserted later; after the Restoration the following note appears—'Register not kept for about 14 or 15 years, all the time of Mr Jeremiah Dike being here'. At St Mary's church, Little Parndon, Mr Haughton entered the baptisms and burials as usual, and also a few marriages. The last of his marriage entries runs as follows: 'April 10, 1656. This yeare and day of ye month was Mr. Arthur Sparke of this parish and Mrs. Mary North of Bromfield maryed by Mr. Champneys of Harlowe according to ye statute'.

The statute referred to legalized a civil marriage by a magistrate in a market-town, the banns having previously been published in the market-place on three successive Sundays or market-days.

Our district was spared the worst horrors of the civil war, for the tide of battle did not reach Essex except for the one action against Colchester. In one of her letters Lady Altham mentions that the trained bands had been mobilized, and there is a tradition that there was a camp on the common, which at that time extended from Harlow to Nazeing, but there was no fighting in this neighbourhood.

When the protectorate was established under Cromwell and a new Parliament elected, one of the members was Edward Turnor of Little Parndon. He came of a family of lawyers, who first appear as owners of Canons. Edward Turnor left Canons for the neighbouring manor of Little Parndon, where Sir Henry Colt had built a new mansion. Henry Colt died in 1631, and his heir George Colt sold the manor of Little Parndon to Turnor. Edward Turnor was a prominent member of the Parliaments of Oliver Cromwell and of his son Richard. He was a member also of the House which voted for the restoration of Charles II. He was Speaker of the first Parliament which Charles II called in 1661, when he addressed the King in terms of fulsome adulation. He received a knighthood, and was appointed attorney to James, Duke of York, the King's brother and successor. Later he became Chief Baron of the Exchequer; he died on circuit, and was buried at Little Parndon; the manor remained in the family for about a century, but Sir Edward's successors made their home at Hallingbury Place.

James Altham was rewarded for his services to his King by a knighthood of the Bath; as a thanksgiving for his return to Mark Hall he restored to the benefice of St Mary-at-Latton the rectorial tithes which had been appropriated centuries before to Latton Priory. It continued, however, to be known as a vicarage, even until today, although it is in fact a rectory.

The incumbents who had been deprived of their livings in 1644 were now restored to their former state, and the intruding ministers were ejected. At Great Parndon, the only living in this district where a sequestration had been effected, both the original rector and the intruder had died, and to the vacant benefice a son of the old rector was presented.

In 1662 a revised prayer-book was issued and a new Act of Uniformity was passed. The clergy who refused to conform were deprived of their benefices. Many Essex ministers were among this number, and much hardship was suffered. In several cases the clergyman so deprived set up a meeting-house where he could continue to minister to his followers; thus the foundations were laid of the nonconformist churches. The first nonconformist community in our neighbourhood was ministered to by William Woodward, who had been deprived of his benefice at Southwold in Suffolk. It is uncertain what drew him to Harlow but tradition says that he had been a chaplain of the forces under the Parliament, and while ministering to the soldiers encamped on the commons had made many friends in this neighbourhood. Woodward did not die till 1712, and the most probable date of the camp would be in 1647 or 1648, sixty-four years before his death. If the traditional story is correct he must have been a very youthful chaplain. The early nonconformist community met under great difficulties, in private houses, or in the seclusion of Parndon Woods. Their first meeting-house was on the border of Great and Little Parndon near the com-

IX Mark Hall in the seventeenth century, reproduced from an old painting

X St Andrew's church, Netteswell and Netteswellbury, from an old photograph

mons; a pasture adjoining Stewards Farm on Commonside Road was called 'Meeting-House Field'. When the Five-mile Act was relaxed the Baptist congregation moved to Potter Street and Old Harlow.

William Woodward bought a tenement and croft called Pottersfield, Foster Street, in 1677. He bequeathed this to Thomas Hawkes—a descendant of Thomas Hawkes martyred at Coggeshall in the reign of Mary—to be used as a burial ground for Baptists. Mr Woodward was buried there and later Sarah Flower Adams the author of several hymns, including 'Nearer, My God to Thee'. Sarah Flower Adams was born in 1805 in a house which still stands in the High Street, and in later years was visited there by the poet Robert Browning who is said to have greatly influenced her poetry. She died in London in 1848, having been a worshipper at Harlow Baptist Church although never a member.

Although there were no ejections in this district, and no deprivations for nonconformity, there were two livings vacant at the Restoration; Jeremiah Dike had died at Great Parndon, and William Haughton at Little Parndon. The new rector at Little Parndon was Henry Wooton. His register is an unusual volume—a large paper-book instead of the standard narrow vellum register, and its contents are very varied and illuminating. In his day this tiny parish on the borders of Essex and Hertfordshire became a sort of local Gretna Green. During the early years of his ministry the marriages only averaged one every two or three years, but they suddenly became very numerous averaging about twenty a year. Many curious notes and items have crept into this register, but perhaps the most interesting record is an ordinary baptismal entry—'Septem: 3 1694: this day Charles the third son of ye Right honorable Edward, Lord Ratcliffe, and ye Lady Mary his wife was borne in this parish; and soone after baptised'.

Edward, Lord Ratcliffe, son and heir of the Earl of Derwentwater, came of the same family as Robert Ratcliffe, Lord Fitzwalter, who sold the manor of Roydon to the foundress of Christ's College, Cambridge. He appears to have leased the manor of Little Parndon which was then called Parndon Park, from the Turnors, and lived there during the closing years of the seventeenth century. His wife was Mary Tudor, a natural daughter of Charles II by Mary Davis. Edward Ratcliffe succeeded to the earldom in 1697, and was followed by his son James in 1705. The young Earl of Derwentwater supported the Pretender, and was one of the leaders in the rebellion of 1715; he was taken prisoner, condemned, and executed. Charles, his younger brother, was also captured and might perhaps have been pardoned on account of his youth, but he escaped out of prison and fled to the continent, where he attached himself to the court of the Pretender. In the 1745 rebellion he sailed for Scotland, but his ship was intercepted off the coast, and he was taken to the Tower of London. There the sentence passed on him thirty years previously was carried out.

Charles Ratcliffe, as his brother's heir, styled himself Earl of Derwentwater, but by a bill of attainder all his titles and honours had been forfeited. Though not legally a commoner and liable to be hanged, drawn and quartered, he was allowed a peer's privilege, and was beheaded on Tower Hill. So of the two brothers, who spent their childhood at Little Parndon, one was executed after the 1715 and the other after the 1745 rebellions.

The seventeenth century witnessed a steady development in domestic building, and it was in this period that the fate of many manor houses was decided; some grew into large mansions with pleasure-gardens, avenues, and parks, while others became farmhouses. During this century Moor Hall, Mark Hall, Little Parndon Manor, Canons, and Netteswellbury were all either rebuilt or much enlarged, and became the seats of the local magnates. Of these only Parndon Hall, the successor to the original manor, survives, while from Canons and Netteswellbury the glory has departed. They were converted into farmhouses and little remains of their ancient dignity except the garden wall and the old barn at Netteswellbury, the timbers and framework of which are thought to be of sixteenth century origin, and the massive brick piers of the great gateway at Canons.

There are, however, many humble dwellings of this period, including a number of small farmhouses, mostly adhering to the same simple plan—three rooms above and three below, with a bold central chimney-stack forming the dominant feature. The main entrance opens straight into the principal apartment—sometimes called 'the house-room'—with its wide open hearth, behind which lies the parlour. The small room at the other end of the building contains the stairway. Upstairs are three communicating bedrooms, the central one for the master and mistress of the house and the one over the parlour for the daughters, while the sons slept at the head of the stairs. Attached to the house there is usually a large one-storey building which served as a brew-house, wash house, etc., and this with some smaller subsidiary buildings helped to enclose a small backyard. Many dwellings of this type, built on a timber frame and plaster-covered, are dotted over our area, some still serving their original purpose, others divided into cottages. The High Street of Harlow affords some examples, for here were once the homes of several smallholders; in spite of the modern shop-fronts the upper portions of several houses still retain their farmhouse character.

Chapter 9
More Recent Times

The principal residence at Harlow in the seventeenth century was Moor Hall, which under the Bugges had become a large country house. It passed into the possession of the Henshaw family, and towards the end of the eighteenth century was purchased by John Perry of Blackwall. Under the Perrys the Moor Hall estate was considerably extended. After the death of his elder brothers, Thomas Perry, the third son of John Perry, succeeded to the property and rebuilt the house in the classical style then so fashionable. As heir to his grandfather George Watlington he changed his name to Perry Watlington and became an important local magnate. He was a very generous benefactor to Harlow, and most assiduous in improving the social conditions and local amenities of the neighbourhood. Under him the Moor Hall cricket club came into being, one of the most celebrated clubs in the county and a notable nursery of Essex cricketers. Today nothing remains of this country house with its lawns sweeping down from the portico entrance to the lake. A small lodge stands on the Matching Road, the last vestige of the manor house that had existed from Saxon times. But the name of Perry Watlington has not been lost: one of the new town's Industrial Health Centres is named after him.

At Mark Hall the royalist squire, Sir James Altham, was succeeded by his brother Leventhorpe, a wine merchant. He died in 1681 and was followed by his son James, who died in 1697. His son and heir, Peyton Altham, held the manor for nearly forty-five years, but the long association of the Althams with Latton was broken when Peyton's heir, Sir William Altham, sold the estate to Sir William Lushington. The Court Rolls of Latton Hall for 1772 were signed by Altham and those for 1777 by Lushington, the change of ownership taking place between those years.

Under the new owner extensive alterations took place; the old house with its ancient hall, its long wings and galleries and its high-walled courtyard was pulled down and a large mansion in a severe eighteenth century style erected on the site. The park was greatly enlarged and included the site of Latton Hall which was completely demolished between 1788 and 1785. When this was done, Latton Street was diverted a quarter of a mile or more to the west of the old line, passing close to the vicarage and leaving the church in a very isolated position. The diverted road then made a sharp bend to regain the old track. This diversion of the road can be seen by comparing the Chapman and André map (pages 88, 89) with the map at the back of the book. Lushington's schemes had not been fully carried through when the manor changed hands once more; in 1785 it was purchased by Montague Burgoyne. The new squire was a younger brother of General Burgoyne, one of the principal figures in the American War of Independence, and popularly known as 'Gentleman Johnny'. Burgoyne completed the improvements at Mark Hall and took a very active part in the affairs of the neighbourhood. He interested himself in agricultural experiments and in stock-breeding. He built kennels at Mark Hall—the field opposite Bromleys is marked on the tithe-map as Kennels Field (the original name being Stackfield), and though he did not hunt the country himself, he persuaded his friend Coke of Norfolk to bring his hounds to Latton periodically. He took an interest in the Bush Fair, and endeavoured to restore the wool-mart there.

It is possible that the old Assembly Rooms which stood on the common opposite Bush Fair House date from this period. The building appears on the Tithe Award Map but was demolished in the 1930s. In the heyday of the Assembly Rooms, dances were held on winter evenings, described as the 'stately waltz or the maddening galop'; the Essex Hounds held their meet there, and also the annual Hunt Ball. In the 1840s the Essex Archery Society met at the Assembly Rooms and in the 1880s, horse races were held on the nearby common.

During the threat of the Napoleonic invasion, when volunteers were being sought for home defence, Burgoyne raised a troop of yeomanry and drilled them in Mark Hall park. He was a parliamentary candidate for the Whigs in the fifteen days' poll in 1810, and was defeated. In 1812 he stood again with Charles Weston (afterwards Lord Weston) who was rather unwilling to run as a fellow Whig with him. Montague Burgoyne did not have a great deal of money to spend on the election for which he was subsequently accused of trying to get to Parliament on the cheap. In his address to the freeholders he declared 'above all he could never lose sight of an efficient and constitutional reform of Parliament, a measure indispensably necessary to rescue the country from its present difficulties and danger', and asking them to 'lay aside all idea of compromising with the Tories'. At the end of the seventh day of the poll Burgoyne received 339 votes against the 1,417 of Houblon and 1,251 of Weston. He decided to withdraw, leaving the others as the successful candidates. Houblon was a landowner in Great Parndon.

In 1819 Colonel Burgoyne, as he was then styled, sold the estate to the Rev Joseph Arkwright, grandson of Sir Richard Arkwright, the famous inventor. Under Mr Arkwright the estate was improved and extended. He was a fine horseman and a keen follower of the hounds; after the death of Mr Conyers of Copped Hall in Epping he became

Master of the Essex Hunt and brought the hounds to Harlow, where new kennels were built on Kennel Common, near to Hubbards Hall.

At Little Parndon the manor remained in the ownership of the Turnor family until the middle of the eighteenth century, when it was purchased by Edward Parson. Edward Parson had married Miss Woodley, the daughter of a wealthy West Indian sugar-planter. He pulled down the old manor-house and built a dignified Georgian brick mansion which stood at the highest point of the park where Princess Alexandra Hospital now stands. It was called 'The Upper House', the original house down by the church and river (shown on some maps as 'The Hall' or 'Old Hall') having long been converted into a farmhouse. Several members of the Parson family are buried in their vault in St Mary's church, Little Parndon, and are commemorated on a large mural tablet. There are also memorials to Mrs Woodley, and to her faithful slave Hester. Of the last-named the entry in the burial register is 'Hester Woodley, a negro-woman, housekeeper to Mr Parson, was buried 16th May, 1767'. Hester's gravestone stands at the east side of the church porch. The burials of two other slaves are recorded at Little Parndon in 1777 and 1787. James Parson, son of Edward Parson, was presented to the rectory of Little Parndon by his father in 1772, but in 1796 he committed the care of the parish to William Day, vicar of Roydon, renowned as an athlete and a pugilist, and went to St Kitts in the West Indies to inspect his plantations. He neither returned nor resigned. Mr Day carried out the duties of the charge until 1805, when at last a new rector was appointed.

For a short time at the beginning of the nineteenth century Little Parndon manor was held by William Smith, grandfather of Florence Nightingale and at one time MP for Norwich. Florence Nightingale's mother Fanny wrote in later years that she 'despised the junketings of Parndon'. The manor was purchased from William Smith by William Kerril Amherst in 1822. The Amhersts were Roman Catholics, and as soon as they took possession of Upper House, the library was furnished as a chapel and was served by a priest from St Edmund's College, Ware. One of the sons of the house, Francis Kerril Amherst, became Bishop of Northampton and in his biography some recollections of his childhood have been collected.

He describes the house and the park, and the friends and familiar scenes of his childhood, in the days of George IV and William IV. Many local characters are mentioned; of the church he says—'The parish church, hard by the mill, was then a miserable structure with one of those starved low spires, not uncommon in Essex'. He mentions Mr Johnson the rector of Great Parndon and his musical family; Philip Johnson, one of the sons, was a frequent visitor at Upper House. He began life in the navy, then felt a call to the ministry; he was ordained and became rector of Netteswell, but he had a passion for music and was an expert violinist, and eventually music absorbed all his time and interest. He lived in London, only visiting Netteswell for the week-ends. He was a member of the orchestra at the great Hyde Park Exhibition of 1851.

In 1834 the Amhersts decided to pull down Upper House and build a new one in the park there, and moved to London in preparation for the demolition work to start. The death of two of their children in the epidemic of cholera during their stay in London changed the plans and they never returned to Little Parndon. After the death of William Amherst, the land remained for several years in the hands of his trustees; eventually it was purchased by Mr Arkwright of Mark Hall, under whom the present Parndon Hall was constructed in 1867 on a fresh site in the centre of the park, Upper House having previously been demolished.

At Great Parndon the manor of Canons, where the Farmers had built a large country-seat, was purchased about the year 1700 by Sir Josiah Child, who came of a wealthy family of merchants. He was succeeded by his brother, who was later created Earl Tylney. The principal seat of this family was at Wanstead, where they built an enormous mansion, with spacious gardens laid out on the most lavish scale, and an extensive park. The whole of the Tylney inheritance passed to Catherine Tylney-Long, a young girl who thus became the richest heiress in England. In 1812 she married William Pole-Wellesley, heir of the Earl of Mornington, and within a few years her spend-thrift husband dissipated the whole of her vast estate. The Tylneys, besides possessing the manor of Canons, had acquired one third of the advow-son of the rectory; this together with the manor was for many years retained by them and afterwards by the Earls of Mornington. They did not, however, reside in the village, and the greater part of the mansion at Canons was pulled down and the remainder converted into a farm-house. Later this manor, with the manor of Passmores, was purchased by Mr Arkwright. With the need for a golf course in the new town, Canons was selected for the site and the buildings were converted into a club house.

When Canons was demolished, the old parish of Great Parndon was left without any residence of importance. Passmores was a pleasant country house of no great size (and is still a private residence); all the other manors were held by tenant-farmers. It was at this time, about the middle of the eighteenth century, that a new property at Parndon came into prominence. Kingsmoor House was never a manor and its origin is obscure, but by the eighteenth century it had become a considerable residence with well-disposed grounds, standing on a slight elevation above the common. Here was the home of the Risdens, and of a branch of the Houblon family. It was later purchased by Mr Todhunter who is commemorated in the stained glass windows in St Mary, Great Parndon. Later it was used as a private school.

Netteswellbury, as we have seen, ceased to be a country-seat when the Martins died out. Soon after it came into the ownership of the Blackmores, lords of Briggens in Hunsdon, the old house was demolished and a farmhouse built in its place. Under the Blackmores an attempt was made to enclose the commons. This was in 1820 when the estate had passed to Thomas Blackmore, a lunatic, in the guardianship of his sister Mary and her husband Charles Phelips. The attempt proved ineffectual, but was renewed in 1851, when the lord of the manor was Charles, son and heir of Mary Phelips. He succeeded in getting an enclosure bill through Parliament, and Netteswell Common, Copshall Common, Tye Green and the Common Field were all enclosed. When his son Charles James Phelips died without issue in 1903, the manor was purchased by Mr Arkwright of Mark Hall. With the acquisition of Netteswell, the Mark Hall estate became an unusually compact and extensive property. It then comprised the Harlow manors of New Hall and Kitchen Hall, the three Latton manors, the manors of Netteswell and Little Parndon, Canons and Passmores in Great Parndon, Marles in Epping, just beyond Rye Hill and a farm in Roydon adjoining Canons. The greater part of this estate lay within what is now the area of the new town. In the 1860s the Arkwrights built a considerable number of new dwellings on their estate, and at Latton village provided an almshouse for two families—now a private residence—and the clock tower which dominates the remains of the village close to the junction of the A.11 and Second Avenue.

In agriculture the chief changes were brought about by the enclosure of the commons, and the gradual extinction of the small-holders. The eighteenth century and the early years of the nineteenth century were prosperous times for the farmer; the price of corn kept mounting, and much waste land was brought under cultivation. Instead of a number of small farms the land was concentrated in a few large holdings; and under enterprising landlords, like Montague Burgoyne and Perry Watlington, new ideas were tried out and better stock introduced.

Before the highways were surfaced in a practical fashion, the soft gravel roads of Essex were unsuitable for heavy traffic and much use was made of water-ways. The River Lea had been navigable from early days, and the water level had been controlled by locks from at least the middle of the thirteenth century. A Waltham Abbey court roll of the year 1271 mentions a stretch of the river between Wormley lock and

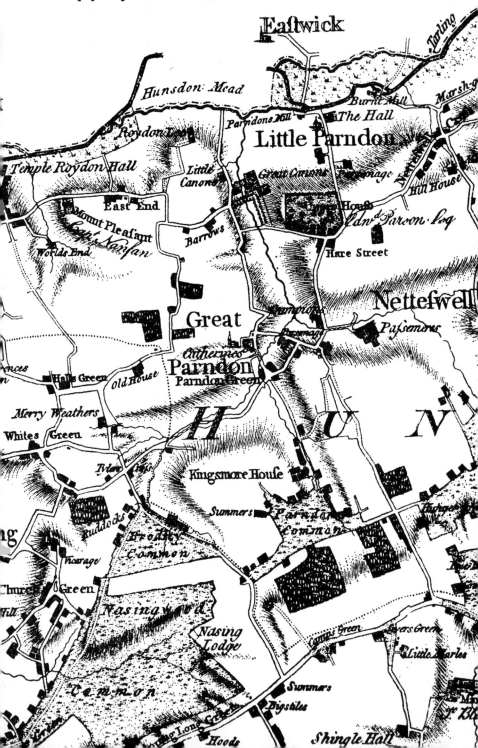

From the map of Chapman & André 1777

River Stort
Harlow Mill
24 M
Eating Bridge
Pincey Brook
W
O

Latton Mill
Harlow Bury
Mole Hall
Houscham

Harlow
Mulberry Green
Pipers
33 M
Church-gate Street

Bromley
New Hall
Harlow Tye
Jackcets

Chantry House
Harlow Tye
Househam Ty

Mark Hall
W.m Luckington esq.

The Hall

Hubert Hall

22 M
Old House
Rauthe.Hall
N

Totts Green
Burs
Thrashers
Hoults

Hall
Roms Street

Latton Street
Kitchin Hall

The Green
Laylands
21 M
Potters Street
Hogs

Bush Common
Magdalen

The Bush
Harlow Park
Qurton
Winters

Latton Park
Harlow Old & Common
S. Ash
Rose

20 M
Paris
Roms
Saw Mills
Greens

Runden
Latton Priory
Canes

Rye Hill

New Hall
Wildin

North Weald
New House

Isgoe

Broxbourne lock. In 1571 a bill was brought before Parliament to improve the navigation of the Lea. The Stort was an insignificant river, and though its flow had been controlled by a series of mill-dams, it was useless as a water-way. About the year 1740 a trust was formed to try and make this river navigable. A canal was cut from mill to mill and a series of locks constructed. The Stort Canal was opened in 1769 and a practicable route for water-borne traffic opened up from Broxbourne to Bishop's Stortford. Hitherto this district had been very self-contained, and such small industries as were carried on only catered for local needs. The enterprise of the Stort Navigation Company and better road communications ushered in new developments; malting and brewing were the first industries to develop along the Stort valley and both of these were soon established in Harlow.

In 1840–1 the Northern and Eastern Railway was constructed along the Stort valley, following closely the line of the canal, and giving direct communication with London and East Anglia. At this date (1841) the town had 2,315 inhabitants, of whom 125 were labourers engaged on the railway. The building of the railway created problems of accommodation for the workmen, some of whom had to sleep in barns. The 1841 Census shows that twelve men were accommodated in this way. The railway was opened to passenger traffic in 1848, offering an hourly service to London which was faster, more frequent and more comfortable than the stage coach, whose disappearance must have been rapid.

When the line was being laid near Burnt Mill one of the workmen was run over by a pilot-engine. He was buried at St Andrew's church, Netteswell, and a score of navvies in their smocks followed the coffin to the church. A century ago all labourers in the country wore the smock, but the last smock in this neighbourhood was worn by an old Potter Street small-holder who died in 1930 at the age of eighty-six.

The opening of the railway led to a steady rise in the population at Roydon and Harlow, at a time when agriculture was waning and the population was decreasing in the rural parts of Essex. The biggest change, however, was at Burnt Mill in the parish of Netteswell where the first heavy industry in this town was established in the eighties. The old flour-mill at Burnt Mill had become derelict and was put up for sale. It was purchased by Messrs Kirkcaldy, a firm of marine engineers from Thames-side. In the quiet water-meadows of the Stort a foundry and workshops were soon established; several rows of workers' houses were built and a new population moved in. Later in 1932 a machine-tool factory was set up at Harlow and about this time several light industries on a small scale were introduced.

But though better communications encouraged new industries and offered improved facilities for commerce, they had an adverse effect on local handicrafts. Some of these were already declining and out-of-date; others were unable to compete with the cheap products of the factories. In all our villages during the middle ages many trades were carried on. Some like those of the carpenter are still in evidence, but the majority have died out. In Tudor times there were still potters, weavers, dyers, glovers, tanners, and many other craftsmen. They have left behind them a number of surnames, and some local names as well. Thus at Harlow 'Glasshouse Field with Glasshouse Cottage attached' which stood at Maypole Corner, recalls the workshop of a glazier, while at Netteswell, adjoining Hill House, was a close called 'Tainter Field'. Hill House was at one time the home of a dyer, and Tainter Field was the ground where he set up his frames furnished with tenter-hooks upon which the cloth pieces were stretched. 'Potter Street' (earlier known as 'Potters Street') was the quarter where the potters dwelt and had their kilns, while 'Tannery House' (now Netteswell House) at Netteswell Cross, adjoined a tanyard which fell out of use more than a hundred years ago. This house contains two very fine carved fireplaces and served for several years as the Treasurer's office of the Urban District Council. At Latton in the middle of the seventeenth century there were several potters, the most populous part of the village being only a few yards from Potter Street. There was also a dish-turner, and a cloth-worker. A house called Pot House was leased in the early seventeenth century to William and John Prentice, potters; the cottages standing at the junction of Pytt Field, Carters Mead and the cycle track may possibly be this property. Some spinning and weaving was practised in all medieval villages, but there is little evidence to show that cloth-making was ever the main industry at Harlow. *The History of Essex by a Gentleman*, published in 1771, says—'The great woollen manufactory which was carried on at this place for many years is now removed; and the poor are principally supported by spinning'. The Gentleman's History is, however, not very reliable and the statement quoted lacks support. Only a century ago tradesmen still sold their own handiwork. There were then in this district several shoemakers, tailors and dressmakers; smiths and tinmen supplied all the metal requisites for farm and kitchen; there were carpenters and saddlers to make furniture and harness, while candles were made and supplied by the chandler. One lady plied the unusual trade of straw-hat maker. A brick and tile works was then functioning in the area, as well as a brewery and more than one malting. By the end of the nineteenth century the list of industries, small and large, in Harlow contained shoemakers, basketmakers, hurdlemakers, coach builders and wheelwrights. A product known as 'Victoria Dry Glazing' was manufactured at Deards Patent Glass Works. However, in the earlier part of the nineteenth century the employment position was serious, for the Minutes of the Epping Union record in 1836 that the number of the labouring classes in Harlow far exceeded the demand. Nevertheless, improved communications later created new jobs. With improved road construction under the influence of MacAdam, and the new vogue of the bicycle, innkeepers and caterers opened their doors to the growing band of cyclists. Locally William Collins started business as a cycle-maker about 1896, probably being a descendant of Harvey Collins, a wheelwright of Harlow in 1816. However, the old trades of saddler and wheelwright continued for some years; a firm of saddlers existed in Fore Street, Old Harlow, until the late 1930s. The introduction of the motor car led to the establishment in 1914 of a firm of motor-engineers by Arthur Sutton of Station Road, Old Harlow, to be followed in the 1920s by Larter and Dearlove's.

Postal services in this area were instituted in the first quarter of the nineteenth century. Initially, the horse-drawn mail coaches provided the transport between different parts of the country, to be replaced by the rapidly expanding railways and, later, by mail motor vans to expedite local deliveries. By 1866 there were three postal deliveries on weekdays in this district with one delivery on Sundays. By 1899 post offices were operating in Harlow, Potter Street, Great Parndon and Netteswell, the latter serving Little Parndon. In 1908 the first public telephone call boxes were established in Harlow, and in the same year, with the growing demand for telephone service, Exchanges were established in Potter Street and (Old) Harlow, the latter having, initially, 17 sub-scribers which grew to 200 by the early 1930s.

In 1862 gas street lighting was introduced into the parish of Harlow, and was gradually extended, not reaching the Sheering Road and Hobbs Cross until 1901. In the other parishes very little street lighting was installed until comparatively recent times. The Harlow and Sawbridge-worth Gas Light and Coke Company built a gasworks in Harlow in 1870. The lighting of streets by gas continued for nearly eighty years when it was superseded by electricity. During most of this time the lamplighter was a familiar sight in Harlow, going on his rounds with his pole at dusk and dawn to light and to extinguish the lamps.

Social life for many centuries had been provided by the churches of the district; the first development of secular social life came in 1887–8 with the building by a private company of Victoria Hall, Old Harlow, used for social functions. It came into the possession of Harlow Parish Council in 1933, was then transferred to the Urban District Council who sold it in 1967 to Essex County Council. It is now used as a youth centre.

A golf club had been established on Harlow Common by 1910 and continued to serve the neighbourhood until the outbreak of the Second World War when the land was put under cultivation. Horse racing was held in Mark Hall Park as early as 1826 on a course laid out specially for the purpose. Annual race meetings were held which continued into the twentieth century.

Prior to the construction of the new town this district was essentially rural, apart from a few industries and shops, tradesmen, and a dying band of craftsmen to serve the small scattered population. The parish system existed as it had done, unchanged for more than a thousand years. The village system too had undergone little in the way of change. As we have seen, the manorial system had broken down, but the landed gentry had replaced the lord of the manor at the top of the social structure. There are Harlow residents still living who can recall touching their caps to 'the squire' when they met him.

Chapter 10
The Old Inns and Taverns

The medieval records of the manors of Harlow make no mention of inns, but it must not be assumed that they did not exist. Prior to the fifteenth century when inns began to be a common feature, especially along the main routes, the religious houses had fulfilled the needs of the traveller, who preferred to stay at monasteries rather than face the horrors of the medieval hostelry. The standards offered by the monks varied as much as hotels do today, but the cooking and accommodation were far better than could be obtained in inns, where often the unruly congregated.

The earliest reference to an inn at Harlow is to be found in the Tilty Cartulary for the year 1444. This records the expenses of Brothers John Dunmawe and John Feryng with two servants going to London. On Wednesday, May 27, John Feryng returning home with one servant had breakfast at Harlow at the cost of one penny. The same monk returning home on June 25 from a second visit spent four pence for dinner at Harlow.

Their route from London to Tilty lay via Tottenham, Edmonton, Waltham, Nazeing, Harlow and Takeley; and whilst the entry does not name the inn it is possible that it was the Green Man, which is one of the oldest inns standing on the route, dating back to the fifteenth century. The Green Man stands at the junction of the medieval road system in Harlow. One road led eastwards to Sheering, Hatfield Broad Oak and Dunmow, westwards to Nazeing, Waltham and London. Northwards the road led to Bishop's Stortford, whilst a track on its western side ran southwards to Potter Street and Epping.

It was not until the seventeenth century that an inn appeared in the Sessions Rolls by name, when in 1602 Richard Staines at the George, Harlow, was charged with buying, selling and keeping beer on the Sabbath.

Three deeds concerning the George dated 1662, 1665 and 1668 are extant from this period. An indication of the lands and buildings attached to this inn are given in the deed dated 1662. It is described as 'all that messuage or tenement with barns, stables, outhouses and buildings, yards and gardens and orchard and bowling green . . . commonly called or known by the name of the George Inn'. The deed of 1665 gives some further information concerning the inn when it states 'the George, alias Lawrence Greenes alias Bakers, with all houses and one orchard called Greenes Orchard . . . one parcel of land called the

Bowling Green, containing 2 acres'. The property at this time covered an area from Fore Street northwards to beyond where Barclays Bank now stands in Station Road and included the ground upon which part of Station Road was built. The present Chequers (Old Harlow) was a dwelling house within the gardens; in 1721 this house belonged to Richard Sharpe under a lease and is described in a deed as being part of the garden ground belonging to the 'George' inn. In a deed of 1777 the house had become two tenements under one roof with a piece of garden attached called Hithergarden 'and situate on the back side of the George inn'.

In the early 1800s, the two inns already mentioned—the Green Man and the George (sometimes called Great George), assumed importance as staging posts for the growing horsedrawn traffic. Kent's *Shopkeeper's and Tradesman's Assistant* of 1812 lists the coaches, waggons and carts for London, peak traffic being on Tuesdays, Thursdays and Saturdays with five coaches, and the addition of three waggons and a cart on Tuesdays, one waggon on Thursdays and two waggons and a cart on Saturdays. It would seem from the old timetables that in 1823-4 the Green Man at Mulberry Green was the principal coaching inn, but by 1839 the George had become the more important of the two. Pigots & Co's Directory of 1839 lists the Royal Mail, Magnet and Telegraph coaches, all bound from Norwich to London, calling at the George every morning. In Paterson's *British Itinerary*, 2nd edition, c. 1800, is a timetable for the Norwich–London mail coach. This left Norwich at 4.30 p.m. and drove through the night reaching Harlow at 3.50 a.m. and London at 7 a.m. taking 14½ hours; on the return journey it left London at 8 p.m., reaching Harlow at 11.16 p.m. and Norwich at 10.45 a.m. the next day, calling at Thetford for breakfast, a total of 14¾ hours.

Other coaches called at the George from Bury St Edmunds, Cambridge, Haverhill, Holt, Norwich, Swaffham and Saffron Walden, some bound for Charing Cross and others for Whitechapel. There was a coach from this inn to London every Monday at 6.30 a.m. and on other mornings (Sunday excepted) at 8 a.m.

It may well be that the horses were changed at the George, but certainly the guard was left with the coach whilst stops were made to protect the coach and the mail. The present guards on trains are the successors of these coach guards.

The decline of the Green Man in favour of the George as a coaching inn was probably the result of the cutting of the road from the George corner to the bridge at Harlow Mill in 1828, saving the longer journey via the High Street, Mulberry Green and Old Road.

The George is now a shop. The Green Man still operates as an inn.

In an early Victorian renovation many of the old beams were covered with plaster. In 1968 this was removed, to reveal the charm of the centuries-old building and to restore its air of the coaching days.

Other early references to alehouses in Harlow occur in the Session Rolls, often for breaking the law; in 1536 John Wreyghte of Harlow was indicted for keeping an alehouse without a licence and in 1567 Ralph Graye, also of Harlow, appeared for a similar offence.

In 1599 William Ayeleye was brought before the Sessions for keeping an alehouse, 'being an inconvenient place for the same and maintaining an evil rule'. This may well be the inn now known as the Horn and Horseshoes, Harlow Common. The name of Ayeleye appears in the deeds as tenant prior to Thomas Fowler in 1768. This inn, outside the boundaries of the town but within the parish of Harlow, appears to have been an alehouse or tavern from at least 1745. One of the owners, James Baker, farmer, publican and miller, changed the name of this house from the Three Horseshoes to its present name and, in addition, he built a windmill in a field at the rear of the house. The Tithe Schedule of 1848 gives the details of the inn. The property then consisted of Windmill Field, Windmill Yard, Horns public house and yard, garden around with a tithe payable to the vicar of Harlow of 14s 9d.

Deeds and the manorial rolls furnish further details of the inns and taverns in the parish of Harlow in the early part of the eighteenth century. In 1718 Joseph Abraham surrendered the copyhold tenement called the Little George, then in the occupation of John Thorne, 'situate and being near the Market Place in Harlow', to George Askew, Abraham having secured this property in 1701. Nearly a century later when this property was sold to a firm of brewers in Hoddesdon, it was described as 'the Crown and lately called or known by the name of the Little George'.

In 1641 an incident occurred at St Mary-at-Latton, when as related in Chapter 8 the bell-ringers removed the rails about the communion table, cast them over the church wall on to Latton Street and finally set them on fire. The statement to the magistrate records that they bought a kilderkin of beer from the Black Lyon, an alehouse in Harlow. This tavern ceased trading in 1791.

The deeds of the White Horse, Old Road, Old Harlow, state that in 1779 a tenement existed on this site known as Barnes, which by 1804 had been converted into two tenements with garden ground, the area being known as Barnes Green. In 1806 the old building had been replaced by a new house or tenements under one roof, for the deed of 1830 describes them as four newly erected messuages. A deed of 1842

XI Netteswell, The Greyhound, from an old photograph

XII The Cock Inn, Great Parndon, from an old photograph

states that this was a beer shop called the White Horse, with land at the rear known as Brickfield at Barnes Green.

In 1722 a tavern called the Wheate Sheafe was granted to Jolly Stone of Harlow and the deed states 'all that customary or copyhold messuage or tenement with ye houses, outhouses, edifices, buildings, barnes, stable, yards, and appurtances, thereto belonging commonly called or known by the name of ye Wheate Sheafe, as ye same is situate and being in Harlowe Towne in ye Middle Row there'. In 1782 when James Langfill was admitted to this property by the lord of the manor it was described as 'late called by the name of the Wheat Sheaf and now the Marquis of Granby's Head'. This change of name occurred prior to 1769 for it appears as the Marquis of Granby in the Alehouse Recognizance Books. It is interesting to note that as late as 1722 the term Middle Row is used, a reference to the *media rengea*, see page 59: The Marquis of Granby is still operating as a public house.

During the period 1715–36 the Queen's Head, Churchgate Street, became a tavern under that name. The will of John Thompson dated 1715 and proved in 1720 mentions two tenements, one known as the Priest's Chamber, and another known as Chamberlines. This last tenement appears in a deed of 1736 as 'a Tenement heretofore called or known by the name of Chamberlines but now called by the name of the Queen's Head'. The sign would appear to be that of Queen Anne. Whether or not this seventeenth century house was an inn prior to the deed of 1715 is not known, but no mention is made of it in the survey of 1431 for this states that the house next to the churchgate was the house of the vicar's chaplain (Priest's Chamber) and next to that the church clerk, from which the name Chamberlines is probably taken. The Queen's Head is still in business as a public house in Churchgate Street, having changed little in outward appearance during its long life.

Another reference to a house which still serves as a public house, i.e. the Red Lion at Potter Street, occurs in 1721 when Richard Lake became tenant under the will of Susannah Lake to one seventh part of 'all that messuage or tenement called the Red Lion, otherwise Cock Potters, holden of the said manor, and also all that workhouse or shed thereto . . . situate at or near Potter Street'. Richard Lake held the whole of the property by 1747, and it remained in the hands of the Lake family until 1822 when it was purchased by a firm of brewers.

Also in Potter Street was another tavern which appears in deeds of this time—The King's Head. In 1740 this was given by Elizabeth Wright to her grandson Joseph Wright and described as a freehold tenement. In his will dated 1797 the house is referred to as 'pulled down by ye said John Wright and a new tenement erected by him on or near

G

the ground or soil whereon the same stood now called the King's Head'. When this house was demolished in 1957 a small prayer cupboard used by recusants was found in one of the rooms. It is now in the hands of Potter Street Baptist Church. The licence was transferred to the new Phoenix in Tillwicks Road though the name has been perpetuated in the King's Head Playing Field at Potter Street.

With the institution of the Alehouse Recognizance Books in 1769, details of the licensee, sign and sureties were listed under the headings of parishes and Hundreds and these continued until 1828 when the registers ceased.

At the time of the commencement of the Registers there were fifteen alehouses entered for (Old) Harlow; the King's Head, the George (actually known as the George IV, Harlow Common), Little George, Great George, Green Dragon, Bull (also known as the Black Bull), Black Lyon, White Hart, Three Horseshoes (now the Horn and Horseshoes), Marquis of Granby, Green Man, White Horse (Old Road), Crown, Queen's Head and Red Lion, also known as the Cock. Only the last seven survive today as public houses.

In the parish of Latton, the Sun and Whalebone and Bush Fair House are recorded; in Netteswell, the Chequers and the White Horse and at Parndon the Three Horseshoes and the Cock.

In the *Trade Signs of Essex* (1887, page 7) appears a list of houses for the parishes of Harlow, Latton, Netteswell and the Parndons, for the year 1789, supplied to the author, Mr Miller Christy, by a Mr G. Creed of Epping. This list, however, conflicts with the Alehouse Recognizance Books for the Harlow parish since it omits the Red Lion, the Crown and the George IV. In the other parishes the lists do not differ.

Several of the taverns ceased trading in the parish of Harlow during the latter part of the eighteenth century. The Little George ceased trading in 1772, the Green Dragon in 1779, the White Hart in 1785, the Bull in 1789 and the Black Lyon in 1791. It would seem that Old Harlow at this time was over-provided with taverns. It may be too that the influence of Wesley and the strict Nonconformist view of this period which frowned strongly on strong drink, had some effect on this slump in the tavern trade. The Baptists who met in a chapel in Fore Street from 1764 no doubt rejoiced mightily at what they would have regarded as a set-back to Satan.

In Netteswell, the White Horse ceased trading in 1802 and the Hare and Hounds started in 1803, lasting until 1812. It is possible that these two names represent the same alehouse operating under different signs. The Greyhound first appears in the Registers in 1810; it is still in business at Netteswell Cross, in the picturesque setting of the Town Park.

At Parndon the Three Horseshoes does not appear in the Alehouse Recognizance Books after 1821, but appears to have re-started trading as a tavern later in the nineteenth century. Both the Three Horsehoes and the Cock are still trading in Three Horseshoes Road, Great Parndon. The Sun and Whalebone and Bush Fair House remain in Latton for the period covered by these Registers, whilst an alehouse known as the 'Cow' was licensed for the years 1817–18–19. Whether or not this house became the old Bull and Horseshoes which is opposite Purkis Farm on the A.11 and some half a mile south of the present house of that name is not known.

Bush Fair House served the patrons attending the fair on Latton Common. Doubtless the closure of the fair in 1879 considerably affected the business and it closed down. It has been a private residence for many years and is now called Bush Fair Farm, having been rebuilt in 1878, but with part of the old building remaining at the back of the newer premises. The Sun and Whalebone is still in business just south of Potter Street, in the fork between the old London Road and the new A.11.

The White Horse at Potter Street was a shop until the mid-nineteenth century. The Post Office Directory of 1859 lists the White Horse, the licensee being Boaz Battell. He appears in the Post Office Directory of 1852 as a shopkeeper at Potter Street. He may have decided to become a licensee during that period, possibly to reap some profit from Bush Fair or to extend his business. This was not unusual for publicans; for example, George Hudson of Parndon is listed in the Directory for 1859 as a beer retailer, grocer, shoemaker and postmaster while other publicans carried on business as blacksmiths, carpenters, etc. The White Horse at Potter Street is still trading.

One public house which does not figure in directories or in the Alehouse Recognizance Books is that of the 'Hare' in Hare Street. It is unusual for an alehouse to be known simply as the Hare. Most are called the Hare and Hounds and probably this house took its name from the Street in which it now stands. The only mention of this house occurs in the Trade Signs of Essex, of 1887. It was then probably a beer shop and therefore was not listed as a public house. The beer shop is the forerunner of the modern off-licence. However, a good deal is known about this property before it became a recognised public house. The property (though not necessarily the existing buildings) was in 1693 in possession of the Manor of Canons 'de Paringdon Magna', and remained in the hands of the manor until 1879 (by which date the manor was only a legal entity). From 1785 to 1879 the property was known as 'Slagsbury', from which the nearby Slacksbury Hatch takes its name. At one time 'Slagsbury' formed part of Barrows Farm, which still exists on the corner of Elizabeth Way and the Roydon Road. In 1879 the tenant, John Akers, paid £54 to the Manor for enfranchisement of the property, described as 'two cottages under one roof', and one month later sold it to the brewers who now own it, for £1,100. Since the brewers would not have bought it unless it was already functioning for the sale of ale, etc., it was certainly a beer shop before it was recorded in the Trade Signs of Essex in 1887. There is a strong local legend among older residents of the town that 'The Hare' was previously known as 'The Donkey' or 'The Kicking Donkey' but documentary evidence of this is lacking. It may be that the earlier beer shop went by this name, or that the inn sign was so badly weathered that the portrayal of the hare standing on its hind legs looked like a kicking donkey.

Another pre-new town inn is the Dusty Miller, standing on the A.414 near to the Town Station. The deeds go back only to 1846, when it was known as the Bakers Arms. When purchased by the brewers in 1873 the name was changed to Railway Inn, becoming the Dusty Miller in the late 1950s. The brewers decided to name it after a fishing fly, as a variation on the trend of naming new town public houses after Essex butterflies.

The development of the new town brought a need for new public houses to serve the housing areas. Harlow Development Corporation in co-operation with the brewers decided to use the names of indigenous butterflies for the new houses, the first of these being the Essex Skipper at the Stow. One exception was allowed from this rule, for the new Chequers, Commonside Road, built a few yards from the old inn which is now a private residence. This carries on a name which may have existed since 1721.

Many of the old inns which survive from the eighteenth century or earlier have been altered internally, but most of them fortunately have retained their external features. The inns on the great turnpike roads had their heyday in the days of the stage coach. Nowadays the motor car is bringing new custom to the fine old inns with which this country is endowed.

Chapter 11
The Old Churches and Religious Houses

The origins of the ancient churches of Harlow are vague and uncertain, but they may well owe their foundation to the labours of the missionary priests of St Cedd in the early seventh century. From their religious houses at Othona and Tilbury these priests, with their bishops, travelled throughout Essex converting the people to Christianity, ordaining priests, and often supervising the building of the rude log huts which served as churches—the sole surviving example of which is at Greensted, near Ongar.

Earlier chapters have made reference to the development of the manorial system, and of the parish system which still exists. The parish system in turn determined the village area (though the dwellings might be scattered where the land was enclosed). Under the manorial system the lord of the manor built the church and appointed the priest, this subsequently becoming a right known as owning the advowson, a right which was usually sold with the manor but which in some instances became separated from it and which sometimes (as happened for a time at Great Parndon) became divided between two or more landowners.

The four parishes which developed during the Saxon period in the area now covered by the town were Harlow, Latton, Netteswell and Parndon, though Latton may at some time have been part of the parish of Harlow.

The first mention of a church occurs in the will of Thurstan dated 1041, to whom reference was made in Chapter 3. In his will he granted to the abbey of St Edmunds the advowson of the church—later known as the church of St Mary and St Hugh, (Old) Harlow. A church must have been in existence before the date of the will, serving the manor of Harlowbury and the village of Harlow. The advowson remained in the hands of the abbey until the Dissolution when it passed into lay hands.

Domesday Book (1085) records a church at Latton with a note that it was served by two priests each appointed by the manors later known as Mark Hall and Latton Hall. The date of foundation of this church is unknown but it must certainly have been of Saxon origin.

When Netteswell was granted by Harold to his foundation of secular canons at Waltham (1060) the grant made no mention of a church. It must be assumed therefore, that a church (St Andrew's,

Netteswell) was later built by the canons to serve the tenants of the manor. The inner arches of the north and south doors would suggest that it was built just prior to the Conquest.

Parndon as we have seen was an important site long before the coming of the Romans, and it may well have continued to be so at the time of the Conquest. However, Domesday Book records a manor but not a church. It is not improbable that the usual pattern of a manorial chapel existed. The base of the tower is laid in the Norman pattern of flints and may date from that time. The earliest mention of the church is contained in a manuscript (Cottonian MS Nero CIII, *c.* 1135) in the British Museum, recording a grant of land at Parndon to the Priory of St Mary, Southwark, by Gilbert de Clare. This records a 'capella' or chapel, which may have been the successor of a Saxon church.

The Norman Conquest brought considerable changes to the Church in this country, which had long enjoyed a considerable degree of independence from Rome. William summoned Lanfranc, a monk from Bec, to the See of Canterbury to carry out reforms and to bring the Church closer to the Papacy. The Sees of bishops were removed from villages to large towns, and the monastic system was extended, strengthened and disciplined. The Saxon churches and monastic buildings were swept away. The Norman lords of the manor built substantial churches, and in the twelfth and thirteenth centuries introduced abbeys and priories, two of which were founded in this area—Parndon Abbey in the twelfth century and Latton Priory in the thirteenth century.

The parish of Little Parndon, with its church of St Mary, was created out of the large parish of Parndon. The church is recorded in Fulk Basset's Register and the Norwich Taxation, *c.* 1250, which records that it had no vicar.

The foregoing is a brief impression of the churches, the abbey and the priory which existed in this area in early medieval times. The churches, often neglected, and largely or partially rebuilt, exist to this day, bearing a valuable part of the history of this town. Parndon Abbey has vanished, but the ruins of Latton Priory still exist to the south of the town. Although the old churches of the town are not of the size and magnificence of Thaxted, they each have a continuing story.

The Church of St Mary and St Hugh, Old Harlow

The old Norman church of St Mary, Old Harlow (of which little original work remains) was cruciform in plan (as it is today), but without aisles. It was considerably altered in the fourteenth and fifteenth centuries, and it was at this time that the additional dedication to St Hugh, Bishop of Lincoln, was added. Harlow Fair was held on the Saint's Day of St Hugh.

The earliest mention of priests serving the church refers to Jordan de Ros, *c.* 1190. In 1324 when John de Stainton was rector, he founded a chantry named after him and endowed it with a house, lands and rents in Harlow, Latton, Great Parndon (of which Maunds Farm formed a part), North Weald and High Laver. The income was to be used to maintain a priest to say mass daily for the souls of his parents, the Abbot of St Edmunds, himself, and all the faithful departed. At the suppression of the chantries in 1547 it was valued at £9 os 10d, when Harlow was described as a 'great and populous town, having about 400 houseling people'.

During the Middle Ages two of the priests of this church were concerned in some dubious acts. In November 1402 and again in the following January, William de Humberstone was pardoned for outlawry in not appearing before the magistrates to answer for various debts. In 1434 Walter Martin, late vicar of Harlow, was granted a pardon, having been indicted for entering the house of John Cook of Tateshale, Norfolk, by force of arms, ravishing Cecilly his daughter, and carrying her off with eight pairs of sheets and two coverlets.

Early in 1708 a fire broke out in the church which completely gutted the building, the damage being estimated at £2,035. Permission was obtained to issue a 'brief', i.e. a collection throughout all the parishes in the country. The Harlow 'brief' begins as follows:

'Harlow Church, 28 April, 1708. A sudden and lamentable fire happened in our Parish Church aforesaid, which in a very short time burned down the same together with the steeple and melted all the bells. We, the said petitioners, not being able of ourselves by reason of the largeness of the fabric and the greatness of the loss—the same amounting on a moderate computation to £2,035 17s 3d, to rebuild, etc.'

Many records of the amounts collected by the various churches are in existence; at Great Parndon 11s 6d was collected, at Tollesbury 8d, at St Lawrence, Reading, 17s 8d. Under the energetic vicar John Taylor, the church was heavily restored, a dome being placed over the crossing and a tower surmounted by a cupola erected at the west end of the church. Between 1878 and 1880 the church was again restored, when some features of the church which had survived the earlier fire were returned to their old positions. The tower at the west end was demolished, and the short spire replaced by the existing tall spire. The church contains the largest collection of monumental brasses in one church in Essex.

The Church of St Mary-at-Latton

In Latton the church now known as St Mary-at-Latton, First Avenue,

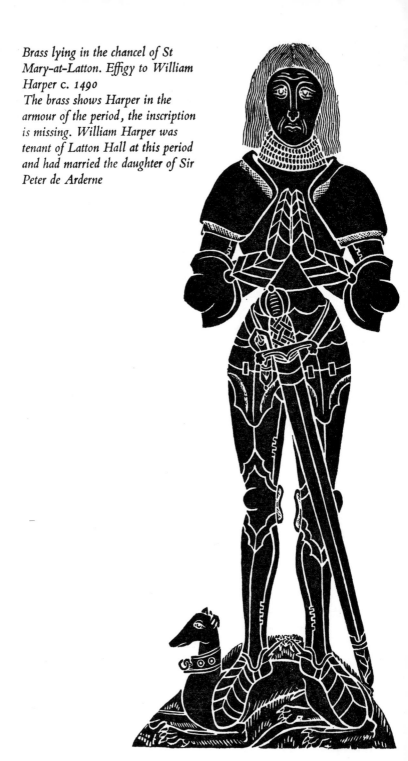

Brass lying in the chancel of St Mary-at-Latton. Effigy to William Harper c. 1490
The brass shows Harper in the armour of the period, the inscription is missing. William Harper was tenant of Latton Hall at this period and had married the daughter of Sir Peter de Arderne

was built close to one of the manors to which it was appended, and some distance from the village. When the Norman lords demolished the old Saxon church a substantial structure was erected. Some indication of this is to be found in the south and east walls where a considerable amount of Roman brick was used as quoins and for facing of arches. Even in those early days the church had a tower, for Ernoldus a chaplain was killed by falling from it in 1234.

During the fifteenth century considerable renovation took place. The tower was rebuilt in Tudor brick, and windows inserted in the walls to lighten the interior. In 1466 Sir Peter de Arderne, Chief Baron of the Exchequer and Justice of the Common Pleas, obtained a licence to build a chantry at Latton. The entry in the Calendar of Patent Rolls, 1461–67, and dated February 10, 1466, states 'License for Peter Arderne, knight, one of the justices of the bench, or his heirs and executors, to found two perpetual chantries, one of one perpetual chaplain to celebrate divine service at the altar of Holy Trinity in the chapel of Holy Trinity and St Mary the Virgin newly-built by him in the church of Latton, Co. Essex, and the other of another perpetual chaplain to celebrate divine service at the altar of St Peter and St Katherine in the same church, for the good estate of the king and his consort Elizabeth, queen of England, and their heirs, and of the said Peter and Katherine his wife, and their souls after death and the souls of the relatives and benefactors of the said Peter and Katherine and all for whom he is bound to pray, to be called the chantries of Peter Arderne, knight'. The chantry chapel, once covered in paintings, has been restored since a fire in 1964 and is now used as a chapel of prayer, dedicated to St Peter.

The Church of St Andrew, Netteswell

The earliest mention of St Andrew's, Netteswell, appears in a charter of Henry II, 1177; a letter of Pope Innocent III, 1199, refers to the churches of Nesinges (Nazeing) and 'Nettesuville' as being built by the canons on their granges or farms. The present church was built at the time of Henry II's charter, and replaced an earlier Norman building of which only the inner arches of the north and south doors survive.

When the Abbey of Waltham was reconstituted by Henry II as part of his penance for the murder of Thomas Becket, Archbishop of Canterbury, a secular canon was allowed to retain the living of the church for his lifetime. On his death his son claimed the living but he was ejected and the living appropriated by the Canons of Waltham Abbey. This is an indication that the principle of celibacy did not always apply during the medieval period.

In the fifteenth century considerable alteration was made to this Early English church. Perpendicular windows were inserted in the walls of the

nave, a belfry tower added at the west end, a wooden porch built on to
the south door, and the church re-roofed. About the same time a small
brick 'rebus' was inserted in the outside wall close to the porch. The
rose which is carved in the centre of the rebus is said to refer to Abbot
Rose of Waltham Abbey 1488–98.

In the seventeenth century internal alterations were made to suit the
form of service then prevalent. A gallery was erected at the west end,
and high box pews and a three-tier pulpit installed. A small lean-to
vestry was built against the north wall. In 1874 a thorough restoration
was undertaken; new pews were installed, the roof and porch renovated
and the old lean-to vestry replaced by the present one. At the same time
the gallery was demolished and an organ—the successor to the village
orchestra—installed. St Andrew's is the only church in our neighbourhood which still possesses its medieval bells.

The Church of St Mary, Great Parndon

The origins of the church of St Mary, Great Parndon, have already been
mentioned. In Archdeacon Foliott's proclamation dated 1198, before
Great and Little Parndon were separated, Godfrey de Parndon is
recorded as priest, the first to be traced. The church is mentioned in
Fulk Basset's Register and the Norwich Taxation, *c.* 1250, as Parndon
Magna, indicating that by this date Little Parndon had become a
separate parish. In this Register the patron is shown as Richard Wytsand,
with the comment concerning the church 'valuation 10 marks, no
vicar'.

The old church was thoroughly restored in the fifteenth century
when it consisted of a nave, chancel, tower and a sacristy on the north
side of the chancel. Later in the sixteenth century a south transept was
added and the south door blocked up, the north porch possibly being
built at the same time. Until the restoration of the tower in 1967 there
was an external and internal door to the stairway of the tower—an
unusual feature. The external door was blocked up when the tower was
restored. The north transept was built in 1913, the gift of Mr J. Todhunter of Kingsmoor House.

Internally there is a lovely perpendicular font and a few remains of
the stained glass that once filled the perpendicular windows. Rowland
Rampston, who died ten years after the Armada, is commemorated by
a monumental brass in the chancel, which records that he 'departed this
lyfe in the faith of Christ and in an assured hope of a happie resurrection,
10th Sept. 1598'.

The Church of St Mary, Little Parndon

The parish of Little Parndon, as already stated, was formed out of the former large parish of Parndon. Like its larger neighbour, the parish has had a number of different spellings. In the Patent Rolls of 1359 it is Little Permdon, in 1486 Little Pardinton, and in the Valor Ecclesiasticus of 1535, Paringdon Parva.

The church was probably founded and endowed by the de la Mare's who had changed their name from de Perendune. The church lay close to the manor-house which they occupied for several generations, but the endowment was so poor that the living frequently remained vacant. Little is known of the church throughout the Middle Ages other than the names of the priests who served it. In 1868 the old church was demolished and the present structure erected through the generosity of Mr Loftus Arkwright and the then vicar, Mr Hemming. In addition, a shilling rate was levied to help towards the cost. The new structure, incorporating one or two features of the old church, was raised on the old foundations, but with an apsidal chancel in place of the square east end of the old church.

Parndon Abbey

Parndon Abbey was an offshoot of Newhouse, in Lincolnshire, the first of the houses of the Order of Premontre, or Premonstratensian Canons to be established in this country in 1143. Parndon Abbey can therefore hardly have been founded before 1160. The earliest mention of the abbey is in 1172 when Robert, abbot of Perhendune (Parndon) witnessed a charter to the monks of St John's, Colchester. When in 1180 the community at Parndon moved to their new site at Beeleigh the canons retained their property at Parndon and used it as a monastic grange, which became known as the manor of Canons. This remained in their hands until the Dissolution. No trace of the abbey remains: Canons Brook Golf Club buildings stand on the site.

Latton Priory

The second religious house was that of Latton Priory which appears to have been founded a little later than Parndon Abbey, probably by Eutropius de Merk, of Mark Hall. The earliest mention of this house which was founded for the Order of Canons Regular of St Augustine— known as Augustinian Canons, or black canons from their habit—is on a bede-roll sent to various monasteries and churches after the death of the first Prioress of Hedingham, to request their prayers for her soul. This bede-roll cannot be earlier than c. 1230.

Because of the poverty of this house, great difficulty was experienced throughout its life in maintaining the community of a prior and four canons, and for most of the period of its existence it was necessary for the Bishop of London to select and install the prior.

The taxation of Pope Nicholas IV, *c.* 1291, gives the income of Latton Priory as follows: 'goods of the Prior of Latton in Storteford, rent 2s; in Gedelestone (Gilston) rent 2s; sum 4s; in Macching 4s; in Latton lands, rents, customs, young of animals, etc. £2 11s 6d; in Reyndon (Roydon) rent 5d; sum £2 15s 11d, Deanery of Angre (Ongar) rent 2s 7d; Alton Laverne (High Laver) rent 1s; Morton rent 5s; North Weald rent 3s 6d; Deanery of Chelmsford from the parish of Chelmsford rent 4s, and the parish of Mulesham rent 4s.' Part of this income had to be remitted to the Pope and was known as the Tenth.

The monastery had at its foundation by the de Merk family become possessed of their portion of advowson of St Mary's church, Latton. Later the other portion was granted to the priory by the de Tany family of Latton Hall. Thus the advowson was held solely by the priory; the rectory was appropriated and a vicarage endowed, i.e. the priory received all the tithes and emoluments due to St Mary-at-Latton, and from these paid a priest to serve the cure. It is possible that one of the canons fulfilled this task and thereby saved the money for the convent.

In 1536 John Taylor, the last prior, left the monastery and it passed into lay hands. A manuscript in the British Museum (Add. MS 6364, f131) dated 1536 records that 'the King by a certain mainprise has committed to John Wentworth, esquire and other, the custody of the site, circuit, and precinct of the Monastery or Priory of Latton, in the Co. of Essex, also the custody of 200 acres etc. To hold for the time of the prise thereof to the end of S. Michael'. Some two years later the King granted the site and lands to Sir Henry Parker, KB, Lord Morley of Great Hallingbury, from whom it passed through various hands until purchased by Sir James Altham in 1562.

A considerable portion of the priory church is still standing south of the town, having been converted into a barn. The four arches of the crossing supported on clustered columns date from the latter part of the thirteenth century. The short transepts have survived and in these the doorways and windows which have been filled in can be traced. One piscina remains. Nothing is left of the choir and chancel, but a short section of the nave has been left and contains a small clerestory window on the north side, some remains of the night-stair by which the canons entered the church from the dormitory, and a door giving access to the cloister on the south. A farmhouse has replaced the old prior's dwelling, the space between this and the church being occupied by the cloister-garth. When a hole was dug in this space some years ago, the coffin of a canon was discovered, suggesting that this area was also used as a monastic cemetery.

It has been the occasional practice over the last few years to hold a

service in the ruins of the priory on the day of the Nativity of St John
the Baptist, to whom the church was dedicated.

The Nonconformists

From Saxon days until the mid-sixteenth century all these churches
recognised the Pope as the Head of the Church. These links were to be
broken in one of the salient developments of our history—the Reformation, an account of which is given in Chapter 7. From the Reformation
until the Toleration Act of 1689 the years were marked by the continuing struggles of the religious factions. Under Elizabeth I the
Puritans, some of whom aimed at the substitution of presbyterianism
for episcopacy, began to hold meetings known as 'prophesyings'.
Because their influence was regarded as dangerous, Whitgift, Archbishop of Canterbury, and Richard Bancroft, Bishop of London,
insisted, with the whole-hearted support of Elizabeth, that all clergy
should accept the Articles, Prayer Book and Royal Supremacy. Those
who refused were deprived of their benefices, some being executed and
others banished or imprisoned.

Under James I the Puritans demanded modifications in church prac-
tices and in the Prayer Book. They wanted the use of the ring in marriage and the sign of the cross in baptism discontinued and the words
'priest' and 'absolution' removed from the Prayer Book. These demands
were rejected, but Bancroft who had succeeded Whitgift at the See of
Canterbury set about the reform of the church. Under him a new
translation of the Bible was prepared—the result being the Authorized
Version which is in use today, though often replaced by the Revised
Version and by more modern translations.

With the defeat of Charles I and the establishment of the Protectorate
the use of the Prayer Book even in private became punishable by
banishment. It was a crime to be married in church or to observe
Christmas except as a fast. A great many clergy were ejected and their
benefices given to Puritan preachers.

Charles II who desired toleration in religion ordered that a conference be held of bishops and the leading Puritan divines to discuss the
revision of the Prayer Book. The conference could not reach agreement
and it was decided by the King that the Convocation of the Church
should revise the Prayer Book. This was issued by 1662 with instructions that all ministers not episcopally ordained by that day, and all
who would not assent, were to be deprived of their benefices. All the
clergy holding benefices in Harlow conformed.

One of the groups of Dissenters (or Nonconformists) which had
broken away from the Church of England became known as Baptists.
It is not known for certain when Baptists first worshipped together in

Harlow, but the earliest records of Old Harlow Baptist Church show beyond doubt that they became an organised body on Christmas Day 1662. The covenanting meeting took place at Campions by invitation of the wealthy landowner, Thomas Hawkes. By that time William Woodward, the ejected Church of England minister, had arrived in their midst from Southwold, and it was under his leadership that the covenanting meeting was held. From that meeting at Campions two Baptist communities arose with Mr Woodward as pastor of both—one in Old Harlow and the other in Parndon. Persecution from the authorities arising from the Act of Uniformity drove both communities into the woods for worship in secret.

The Baptists of Great Parndon in later years moved to Potter Street, and their first chapel still stands as a classic example of Nonconformist architecture of the eighteenth century, being opened in 1756. A building of similar design used to stand in Fore Street but this was pulled down and replaced by the present chapel in 1865.

It was typical of the very strict moral and religious principles of the early Baptists that members who departed from their accepted principles were disciplined by being 'publicly cut off in the presence of the whole congregation'. An early entry in the Church Book of Potter Street reads 'Mr Robert Stone was dealt with as above for immoral conduct, carried out the next Sunday'. Later, in 1779 and in 1804, the minister drew up articles of faith and practice which were used as a covenant for those seeking membership. By the middle of the last century the members were involved in controversy on the questions of Open or Closed Communion, i.e. whether or not to admit to the Lord's Table persons who have not received baptism in accordance with Baptist principles, and whether they were to be Particular or General Baptists, (related to the doctrine of particular redemption). As a result the minister left the church in 1886 for a closed communion church rather than accept the open communion practised at Potter Street.

Some indication of the area from which the Baptist Church drew its members is contained in the list for 1876. Of the thirty members, seventeen came from Potter Street, six from North Weald, and one from each of the parishes of Netteswell, Parndon, Stanford Rivers, Magdelen Laver, High Laver, one from Harlow Common and one from a parish not shown. Most of these people would have walked to and from church.

Subsequent years were difficult ones for the community, and it seemed that the chapel might have to close down. With growth in membership following the rise of the new town, the chapel has once again become a living force.

Until the advent of the new town, Harlow possessed neither a

Congregational nor a Presbyterian church, but adherents of other Nonconformist denominations were accepted as members among the Baptists. One Presbyterian family in fact held high office in Harlow Baptist Church for over 140 years. Some doctrinal differences of opinion were the main cause of several members breaking away about 1880 and forming themselves into another church. This was the beginning of Methodism in Harlow eventually leading to the High Street Methodist Chapel being built in Old Harlow in 1886. This was followed by the building of a fairly substantial chapel in Spring Street, Burnt Mill, in 1891, later demolished. However, as explained in Chapter 13, the Methodists were the first denomination to build a church in the new town—St Andrew's church in The Stow.

The Roman Catholics
From the time of the Reformation the Roman Catholic Church experienced great difficulties, its adherents facing persecution and death, for despite legislation which compelled them, as it did the Nonconformists, to swear oaths of allegiance to the King as Head of the Church, they continued to hold to their beliefs. During the period 1580–90 the Session Rolls for this district contain numerous presentments of people who refused to attend the Church of England. For example, at Great Parndon, Hugh and Alice Worsley were presented for not attending communion and ultimately a warrant was issued for their arrest. However they appear to have fled, for when the warrant was presented it was stated that they were not to be found 'in the Bailwick'. A little later (in 1625) it was noted that John Fynch and his wife, and Andrew Fynch, of Netteswell 'are popish recusants and do not repair to the parish church'.

It would seem that the members of the Roman Catholic faith gradually died out in this area, for the Bishop of London's enquiry in 1705 does not list a Papist as being resident. Similarly in 1715–45 when Catholics had to register their estates none are shown for this area. It was not until 1822 when Mr Amherst purchased Upper House that a Catholic family was known to reside here. When the Amherst family left Little Parndon for London in 1834, and for the next sixty years until Mr Newman Gilbey became tenant of Mark Hall, there is no evidence of Roman Catholicism being practised here. Under the Gilbeys, Mark Hall became a centre of Catholics in the area; a chapel was built in Mark Hall, and after the 1914–18 War the house became a centre for the Apostolate of the Sacred Heart. In 1943 the Gilbeys left Mark Hall, but made provision for mass to be said at the Drill Hall, Old Harlow. In 1951 they built a temporary church in Old Harlow in memory of Mr and Mrs N. Gilbey. This was the first church of the

Roman Catholic faith to be built in Harlow since the Reformation, and marked the revival of the Catholic Church in the town.

The Church of St John the Baptist, Old Harlow

During the nineteenth century two new Anglican churches were built in Old Harlow and Potter Street respectively. Both were established as a result of the Oxford Movement, the main aim of which was to restore to the Church of England the dignity and devotion of early church life. The first of the new churches was St John the Baptist, Market Street, Old Harlow. In 1839 the foundation stone of the church was laid by John, Marquis of Bute and Earl of Dumfries and the grey brick church was completed and dedicated in 1840. The church is built in an Early English style, and consists of a chancel, nave and western tower containing two bells. In 1898 a vestry was added. In 1857 the church was endowed and became a separate parish, but was re-united to the parish of Harlow in 1923.

The Church of St Mary Magdalene, Potter Street

In Potter Street a small chapel-of-ease was founded by the Rev Charles Miller, vicar of Harlow in 1834. The building was a poor structure of lath and plaster, almost square with a shallow roof nearly hidden behind mock battlements. By 1888 a larger building was needed, the east wall of the chapel being demolished, a chancel built, and the old east window incorporated into the south wall of the choir. In 1893 the remainder of the old chapel was demolished and the nave built to match the chancel in the Decorated style of architecture. In 1894–5 the tower was added, leaving the church substantially as it is today. In 1865 the area of Potter Street and Harlow Common was made a separate parish, and the church of St Mary Magdalene became its parish church.

All Saints' Mission Church, Foster Street

In addition to these two new churches a small mission church was built at Foster Street, known as All Saints' Mission Church, at the cost of the Rev Francis Richard Miller, vicar of Kineton, Warwickshire. The church was never consecrated, services have been discontinued, and the building is now derelict.

The new parishes

With the coming of the new town, the ancient parish boundaries needed drastic revision to meet the new pastoral situation confronting the Church of England. Instead of the long narrow strips running north and south each with a small frontage on the River Stort, which suited the early agricultural needs of the area, the parishes were all given new

XIII Latton Priory, now used as a barn

XIV Churchgate Street showing the Stafford almshouses and the Queen's Head. The tablet over the door of the almshouses reads 'Given by Julian the wife of Alex. Stafford, Esq., for the habitation of two poor widows of this Parish A.D. 1630'

and compact shapes in 1957. Old titles and parish churches were retained, except that the parish of Little Parndon received large portions of the parishes of Great Parndon and Netteswell and was renamed the Town Centre Parish, with St Mary's, Little Parndon, becoming a chapel-of-ease; the reshaped parish of Netteswell was renamed Tye Green, with St Andrew's as a chapel-of-ease. The parish of Harlow Common received the long southern portion of Latton parish.

The area now covered by the town of Harlow has witnessed many changes from the time when log huts provided the only places of worship. Today virtually all the churches have buildings within the town, while other religions have established their own places of worship.

Chapter 12
The Development of Local Government

Some attempt must be made to trace the rise of local government and the establishment of social services. In medieval days law and order were maintained through the manorial courts; food and drink was inspected, vagrants and undesirable persons expelled from the manor, highways, bridges and watercourses maintained, and a measure of security and protection assured to the tenants. The care of the sick, aged and destitute was often left to the church, the parochial clergy and the monks each taking their part, assisted by many bequests and gifts from charitable laymen; the church too was responsible for what educational facilities were available. All these services were altered or disrupted by the upheavals of the sixteenth century. By that time the manor was already declining in importance, and the manorial courts were concerned with little beyond estate management, much of their authority having devolved upon the justices of the peace. Following the dissolution of the monasteries most of the monks after receiving pensions were granted 'capacities' or dispensations from their monastic vows and they became secular clergy; of their servants many were retained by the new owners of the estates of the religious, though doubtless some were made homeless and unemployed. The problem of vagrancy common during the latter medieval period did not become really acute until the latter part of the reign of Elizabeth I. The parishes of this district lay off the main thoroughfares but it had its share of vagrants as the following entries in the church registers testify:

Latton   1582   'A poor walkinge woman, her name unknowne, was buried the 29 of Julie.'

Netteswell   1585   'The 20 of Februarie was Henrie Dobine baptised, the sonne of wandering persons, William and Elizabeth.'

Netteswell   1587   'The 12 of April was Grace baptised, the child of a beggar-woman delivered at Goldsmiths, (Tye Green) and this childe was buried the 20 of April.'

Netteswell   1590   'The 17 of Januarie was baptised Edward the child of a beggar-woman delivered at Netteswell-berie.' 'The 22 of Januarie was Frances Browne, a beggar-woman buried.'

Great Parndon 1596 'There was buried a poor girl, name not known, found dead in the highway.'

No real solution was found to deal with the problem of vagrancy, despite various attempts by Parliament to come to terms with the problem. The unfortunate wanderers were passed on from constable to constable until they were returned to their native place. They were whipped and harshly treated, and nowhere allowed a lodging. It was only in the nineteenth century that the work-houses made provision for casuals. The constables were supposed to report the vagrants who had passed through their hands, but few of their records have survived. An Essex vagrancy roll for the year 1567 does, however, exist; these are a few entries of the parishes of this district:

'Richard Radman punished like a vagabond at Harlow, 21 March, was delivered by Roger Clarke, constable of Harlow, to John Johnson, constable of Roydon, to be conducted to Temple Colne in Shropshire, where he saith he was born. Hugh Caster and Elizabeth his wife with 4 children was delivered to me, Roger Clarke, by John Stanes, constable of Sheering, whom I delivered to Richard Sprangler, constable of Hastingwood, to be conducted to Bristowe (Bristol) where he saith he was born, 8th August.'

'Richard Partridge, a rogue apprehended by Thomas Wood, one of the constables of Netteswell, 2 September, and whipped according to the statute, and licensed by the high constable to depart into his country, and delivered by Wood to John Hellam, constable of Little Parndon, and Hellam delivered him to Richard Spenser. Also Thomas Rime of Great Parndon received a rogue called Thomas Goodwin, 21 September, and delivered him to Thomas Wood of Netteswell; or else all things is well, we know none offenders.'

Vagrants could be whipped out of the parish and directed to their native place, but for the local poor some provision had to be made. By a statute of the year 1597 the church wardens were made the Poor-Law authority, and the vestry meeting which annually appointed the church-wardens was now empowered to appoint two overseers of the poor to assist them. The new Poor-Law authority was bidden to provide for the poor of the parish by finding work and shelter; thus the village poor-houses came into being. On a blank leaf of the earliest Netteswell register there is a transcript of the copy of court roll by which Jerome Weston, lord of the manor of Netteswell, granted to John Bannister, (whose brass lies in St Andrew's church, Netteswell), Thomas Gray-goose, John Wood, William Hudson, John Clarke, and Nicholas Baker (the principal inhabitants of the parish) a piece of waste land on Tye Green with a cottage built on it for the use of the poor, at a quit-rent of one penny a year. The conveyance was made June 27, 1599. The poorhouse is marked as such on the tithe-map and is still standing. It served its purpose until 1835 when a number of parishes joined together and formed the Epping Union, now St Margaret's Hospital. No doubt the other villages in the district made some similar provision. In several parishes the rent of fields went towards the upkeep of the poor; at Latton a field was known as Poorhouse field, and in Parndon several fields contributed to the poor of Hunsdon village. The Great Parndon burial register records in 1613 'Anne Wright, almeswoman, was buried', and in 1617 'Joan Foote of the Almshouse was buried'. Almshouses were established by the generosity of charitable benefactors to provide free lodging for aged people. Three separate almshouses were founded at Harlow, and Mrs Martin, widow of William Martin, built one at Netteswell in 1746, but these were all somewhat later than the Parndon entries. About a century later the churchwardens allowed the Netteswell almshouse to lapse back into the manor, to avoid the cost of putting it in repair.

The Vestry became more and more important, and in the seventeenth and eighteenth centuries was the principal organ of local government, answerable in most matters to the justices of the peace. It elected at its annual meeting two churchwardens, two overseers of the poor, two surveyors of the highway and one or two constables. These officials were not paid, but for the expenses of the tasks which they undertook they were empowered to levy a rate which had to be submitted to and approved by the justices. The number of rate-payers was not large, farmers for the most part, with the more substantial villagers such as the miller, the smith and the local tradesmen. These comprised the vestry-meeting, which usually resolved itself into a village oligarchy. Besides the voluntary officers, there were certain paid officials such as the beadle and the watchmen. A presentment at the Quarter Sessions in 1584 records that two watchmen, appointed by the constable at Harlow, were set upon by several men, with the result that one of the watchmen was wounded by a pike so that his life was despaired of.

In some cases the constable was still elected at the manor-court, as were some other minor officials, but there was no uniform practice in the matter. In (Old) Harlow as late as 1564, the manor elected William Colloppe and John Davy as leather-searchers, their duty being to see that no hides were sold that had not been properly tanned. But in time most controls and matters of supervision were left to the Vestry.

For the maintenance of law and order each parish was expected to provide a cage, or lock-up, a pair of stocks, and a whipping-post. Most of these have long disappeared, but some residents can remember the Latton cage standing at Bush Fair House.

The chief parish expense was the care of the poor, and the bulk of the rates was levied for this purpose. The overseers' accounts for most of the villages in this district are extant from the end of the seventeenth century, and show how these officials carried out their duties in feeding, clothing, and finding occupation for the poor and helpless. Frequently a woman was paid to come in and nurse a patient, and occasionally a doctor was sent for from (Old) Harlow. The burden on the rate-payers was somewhat relieved by charitable gifts and bequests. Harlow was particularly rich in charities; Francis Reeve, William Newman and Julian Stafford (the wife of Alexander Stafford) each founded alms-houses during the seventeenth century. The Stafford Almshouse still stands in Churchgate Street, as does Newman's Almshouse. The Reeve's Almshouse stands on the Sheering Road near the junction with the Oxleys. For the relief of the poor, John Godsafe, vicar of Harlow (1586–1601) left a tenement, a garden and 2 acres of land in Harlow Town, George Benson 1642–43 left a farmhouse, with barn and several closes of land 'to provide seven poor persons 15s. each to provide for every man of them a jerkin and a pair of breeches and for every woman a waistcoat and petticoat of cloth, marked with the letters GB'. As late as 1840 the will of Edmund Goodwin contained a bequest of £100, the interest to purchase bacon for the poor. Several other bequests were made towards the maintenance of the church and education. At Latton, an old city friend of James Altham, the purchaser of Mark Hall, on retiring from business, settled at Latton Hall. This was Emmanuel Wolley, who left a bequest to the poor of Harlow, Latton and Nettes-well. At Great Parndon, John Sealy, who died in 1589, left £5 a year to the poor of the parish.

Some expense was incurred in the maintenance of the highways, but usually the owners of the adjoining land carted gravel when needed. The highway surveyors appear to have done their work efficiently enough, though there are occasional presentments at Quarter Sessions about the condition of some length of roadway, as when in 1638 the inhabitants of Netteswell were presented for not mending their highway between Burnt Mill Pool and John How's yard. Bridges, which like the roads were subject to inspection and presentment to Quarter Sessions, were the liability of certain individuals. Sometimes it could not be clearly ascertained who was responsible, as in 1568 when the justices had to confess concerning the bridge between Harlow and Weald parishes 'who should make it we know not'. In 1621 it was presented that 'the common footbridge called Parnells Bridge is in great decay, it should be repaired by Richard Hanchet, farmer of Harlowbury and the Parsonage'.

Beyond some medical supplies for the inmates of the poorhouse, little is apparent in the way of health services, but some attempt was

made under the threat of a severe epidemic to isolate the dangerous
cases. Pest-houses, either permanent or temporary, were established,
usually a pair of cottages standing some way out of the village. Two
cottages at Hobbs Cross served this purpose for Harlow, and were long
known as the pest-houses. Outbreaks of plague recurred several times
during the sixteenth and seventeenth centuries, though the terrible
plague of London in 1665 does not seem to have reached this district.
By the beginning of the eighteenth century the most dreaded epidemic
was smallpox; this was first noted in the local registers in 1708 when
'John Gladwin, butcher, who dyed of the smallpox at Pye Corner was
buryed at Netteswell, the 9th of November'. In the next three months
there were six more deaths by smallpox at Netteswell. At Little
Parndon 'William Perriman (a stranger who died of the smallpox) was
buried, August ye 10th, 1761'.

   Until Victorian times there were no local registrars. At the Reformation instructions were issued to the clergy to keep a record of all
baptisms, marriages, and burials; the earliest extant church registers date
from 1538. In 1547 every parish was required to keep a register-book,
but the nature of the book was not specified, and apparently the entries
were at first made in paper note-books, and in haphazard fashion. A
statute of the year 1597 ordered each parish to obtain a vellum register
into which any earlier records were to be copied, and then be regularly
entered up. Latton, Netteswell and Great Parndon all possess the
register procured under this statute, and contain entries dating back some
fifty years previously. These earlier entries were usually copied in from
the paper-books by professional scribes who toured the country for this
purpose, but sometimes, as at Netteswell, the copying was undertaken
by the incumbent. Each page of the entries thus copied in was certified
as correct by the churchwardens. The Harlow registers survived the
fire at St Mary and St Hugh's church in 1708, but were stolen in 1814,
and have never been traced. At Little Parndon the first extant register
dates from 1621. Births are not registered, but as baptism was usually
conferred within three weeks of birth, this was considered a sufficient
record. Unfortunately church registers cannot safely be relied upon as a
basis for statistics; they were not always kept regularly and con-
scientiously by all incumbents. Robert Osboldston at Great Parndon
was notably negligent. Apart from the evidence supplied by registers
as to birth-rate and mortality, many unexpected facts come to light. For
instance, it is only from the registers that we realise that a number of
London children were sent out into the country in the reign of Elizabeth
I and her two successors. The burial registers of Latton, Netteswell and
Great Parndon record with great frequency the deaths of nurslings and
little children from London. Sometimes the full entry is made with

parents' names and the London parish; often all details, even the name, are omitted. Here are some examples:

At Latton from 1586 to 1589 there are eight burial entries, five of them London children. In 1599 appears this record 'Henrie the sonne of a father unknown, a London nurse-childe, buried ye 5 of January'. At Great Parndon in 1617 we find 'Dennis Davy of London, Nurse-childe, buried', while in 1556 'Edward, a nursling, whose surname unknowne' was buried.

At Netteswell in 1593 there was buried 'Robert Bland, the childe of a Londoner'; in 1594, 'the 10 day of June was John Moore buried the child of one of Ratcliffe by London'; in 1597, 'the 9 day of October was Elizabeth buried, the daughter of a Londoner'; and in 1609, 'the 3 of Feb.: was —— the sonne of a Londiner buried'. Even the Little Parndon register, though commencing somewhat later, has this entry 'Anno 1636. Septemb: 2. In this yeare and day of ye month was John Lavender, ye sonne of John Lavender of Bowe neare London, a nurse-child of Philip Graylinge buryed'. The registers only take note of such of these nurse-children as happened to die, these presumably being only a small percentage of those boarded out. Some may have been sent into the country by private arrangement, but it appears probable that many were evacuated by the poor-law authority.

The parish constable no doubt dealt summarily with vagrants, and small breaches of the peace; anything of a serious nature was brought before a neighbouring justice who could commit the offender into custody or accept bail for his appearance at Quarter Sessions. Petty Sessions were not held in this district until early in the nineteenth century. The assize judges dealt with serious crimes, but most offences were presented at Quarter Sessions and the case there disposed of. Thus, in 1598 Robert Crane and Humphrey Bygley, of Harlow, labourers, were accused of stealing a sheep, worth 10s, belonging to John Bearde, of Netteswell. Robert was found guilty and hanged, while Humphrey was acquitted. About the year 1850 Mr Perry Watlington built a police station and court-room near the ford opposite New Hall. The new police had not long been established in Essex, and the buildings which Mr Perry Watlington presented to the county became their local head-quarters. Here too were held the Petty Sessions. In 1908 a new police station and court-house were erected in London Road, Old Harlow, the old building becoming a private residence. In 1957 the present buildings in the Town Centre were opened to succeed those at Old Harlow.

The nineteenth and the first half of the twentieth century were for this district a period of slow transition from a system under which the landowners provided most of the services and left bequests for the care

of the destitute, to a system whereby public authorities became responsible. The Vestry committees were followed by Parish Councils who
were the local authorities until the formation of the Urban District
Council. One of the primary concerns of the Vestries and the Parish
Councils was for the poor.

In 1785 the parish of Harlow adopted a resolution entitled 'Provisions
for the Better relief of the Poor^e in the Hundreds of Ongar, Harlow and
Waltham', having four sections. The committee responsible for carrying out the provisions was empowered in one section to purchase stocks
of wool, hemp and flax, and to set up a spinning room for the instruction of paupers. The last section empowered the Justices 'to send to the
House of Correction, or common gaol, such as shall not employ themselves to work'.

In 1835 when under the Poor Law Act the parishes of Harlow, Latton,
Netteswell and the Parndons joined with other parishes to form the
Epping Union, the workhouse at Harlow was used to house the able
bodied men, with the women and children being sent to Chigwell and
the infirm to Epping. For the purpose of outdoor relief Harlow was
made the district office. Much of this relief was in the form of a weekly
loan until the recipient was able to obtain work. In 1836 James Bennet
was given six loaves and a loan of two shillings and sixpence to support
his wife and six children. At this time it was decided to build a mill at
Harlow for which the motive power would be provided by eight or
sixteen men.

In 1839 the Epping Union opened the new workhouse at Epping in
which ultimately all paupers were accommodated. Conditions were
little better than in the previous houses, and as late as 1865 the Guard-
ians had to grant £1 for clothing to an inmate of sixteen years of age
who had been in the workhouse since the age of four.

In 1858 the Poor Rate in Harlow was 9d in the pound, this being
collected by officials appointed by the Vestry. Gas lighting and other
rates were levied on the valuation set by the Poor Rate. At the end of
the nineteenth century pauper children were boarded out, and many
attended Fawbert and Barnard School.

As far as education is concerned there is little definite evidence in this
district before the eighteenth century. Chantry-chaplains, who had
much time on their hands, were expected to teach and the chaplain of
the Stanton chantry in St Mary and St Hugh's church, Old Harlow,
certainly did so. When the chantry was dissolved in 1548, and the
question of a pension for the chaplain, William Butler, arose, it was
stated in his favour that 'he is of the age of 60 years and of good learning, having none other provision, and teacheth a school in the said town
of Harlow, and is of good conversation'. Apparently the school

collapsed with the dissolution of the chantry and the sale of the chaplain's house. There is no other mention of any school before the reign of Charles I. About the year 1633 or 1634 Lady Altham writing to her son, an undergraduate at Sidney Sussex College, Cambridge, asks 'Could you bring some pretty civil young scollar downe with you that would be willing for his diet this summer to teach your two brothers, who else I am afrayde will much loose there time, by reason Mr Denn hath given over scole, finding himself not fitt to discharge that and his other business?' Thomas Denn was appointed vicar of Latton in 1600, and was preferred to the rectory of Netteswell in 1634, when his son Thomas succeeded him at Latton. It was probably the son who kept the school until he became vicar of Latton. In 1640 Hezekiah Jocelyn kept a school at Harlow, but there was no public grammar-school nearer than Bishop's Stortford. No doubt there was always some private establishment at Harlow in the years that followed, but none is mentioned until the latter part of the eighteenth century, when James Brown, pastor of the Baptists' meeting-house at Potter Street from 1775 to 1803, is stated to have kept a seminary at Harlow for the tuition of young gentlemen. In 1820 Thomas Finch preached a funeral sermon for Mr and Mrs Josolyne of the Chantry House Academy, Harlow. They had died within three weeks of each other in the early summer of that year. The preacher mentioned that Mr Josolyne had kept his school for nearly forty years. About the year 1830 Bishop Amherst in the recollections of his childhood at Little Parndon states that he had two cousins at Mr Tweed's school at Harlow.

About the middle of the nineteenth century a boarding-school was established in connection with St John's church at Harlow; this developed into Harlow College which recently closed down. The old college buildings behind the church have now been demolished.

The first provision for elementary education was under the will of William Martin of Netteswellbury, made in 1711. In this he left sufficient funds to build and maintain a school for twenty scholars, but the bequest was not to take effect until after the death of his widow. Mrs Martin outlived her husband by 65 years, and it was not until the year 1777 that the testator's wishes were carried out. The original school building is still standing close to Broadfield School and is known as Church House.

It was not until the nineteenth century that any provision was made at (Old) Harlow. About the year 1810 a 'British School', i.e. a school to be conducted on non-sectarian lines, was established. This school received a bequest of some £8,000 under the will of George Fawbert of Waltham Cross, whose executor was John Barnard of Harlow. This was in 1836, when the school was rebuilt and its name changed to 'The

Fawbert and Barnard School'. It was enlarged at the end of the nine-teenth century.

Mr Millar, the vicar of Harlow, disagreed with the management of the original 'British School' on the question of religious teaching, and was instrumental in founding a 'National School', i.e. a school founded on the religious principles of the Church of England. This was estab-lished in 1816 at Churchgate Street, adjacent to the church of St Mary and St Hugh. Wright, in his *History of Essex*, records that the school was for 'the children of the laborious part of the population'. A new build-ing, the gift of Perry Watlington, replaced the old school in 1850, and is still in use.

Another 'National School' for twenty-five boys and twenty-five girls, built on waste land adjacent to the church of St Mary Magdalene on Harlow Common, came into use in 1835. The Trustees paid to the manor a rent of 6d for the use of the land. The school was rebuilt in 1885 on land donated by Mr Loftus Arkwright. Nearby at Potter Street, White's *County Directory* for 1848 mentions a grammar school described as a respectable boarding house kept by Mr Peter Cleary, which may be the house known as Kingsdon Hall.

At Great Parndon the then rector Mr Sims wrote in 1834 that 'on entering upon the duties of this parish a year ago I found no school but a weekly one for girls . . . The cottage in which the school is kept is neither large enough nor sufficiently well situated for the purposes of a Sunday School.' Mr Sims built a brick school-room for twenty-five boys and twenty-five girls, at a cost of £65 and an annual charge for the schoolmaster of 'about £25 exclusive of books'. Financial help was given by, and the school affiliated to, the National Society. This building no longer exists: in the 1860s a new school, catering for seventy to eighty children paying school fees was opened, a teacher from Hockerill College being appointed at an annual salary of £30. This building, since extended, still stands in Peldon Road: it was the direct forerunner of Jerounds School.

A small village school at Latton was provided by Mr Arkwright of Mark Hall and stands just south of Coppings, Puffers Green, Latton village, being known as School House. It was superseded by the large schools built to accommodate the children of Potter Street and Latton. About a century ago, Thomas Natt, son of a former rector of Nettes-well, opened a school for the children of the southern part of the parish at 'The Hermitage', Tye Green. This was closed when the Martin school was enlarged.

In 1856, mainly through the generosity of Mr Perry Watlington, a reformatory school was established at Harlow Tye. It accommodated twenty pupils, and was run on what were then considered very modern lines, not unlike the present approved schools.

The late eighteenth and early nineteenth centuries witnessed a great improvement in transport and better communications with London and the chief East Anglian markets. Highways, which had received little attention since the days of the Romans and which in winter were well nigh impassable for wheeled traffic, became the subject of many Parliamentary bills during the seventeenth and eighteenth centuries though these did not always have the desired effect. Later, trusts were formed to put main roads into repair, levying a toll upon the users. The road from Woodford to Harlow Common was maintained by the justices, using funds provided by Acts of Parliament in 1707, 1723, 1742 and 1768. The turnpike trust responsible for this section of road appears to have been set up in 1769. Northward from Harlow Common the main road followed the old road through Potter Street, then along the line of what had been called 'New Street' but emerging near the George corner at Old Harlow, turning eastwards to Mulberry Green (along what is now termed High Street), thence north along what is appropriately named Old Road, to cross the River Stort near Harlow Mill. The Hockerill Trust formed in 1744 which was responsible for the section of the highway from Harlow Common to Bishop's Stortford constructed a new road from the top of the High Street to Harlow Mill. After some controversy the line of the road was agreed upon: a house on the eastern side of the George Inn was demolished, the road being built over the site, over the fairground and some ploughlands called Mill Field, to join the old road near where it crossed the River Stort at the mill bridge but crossing the Stort by a new bridge built twenty yards west of the old one. The road was opened in 1831. The portion of the road from Potter Street to Harlow Mill Station was by-passed in 1961 with the construction of the new road.

By the middle of the nineteenth century roads were again a source of great concern to the authorities. By 1866 the Hockerill Trust was faced with decreasing income from tolls due to competition from the railway, and proposals were placed before the Harlow Vestry to take over the section of road within the parish. This was unacceptable to the Vestry who took the view that the burden on the parish would be too great and that tolls could still pay for upkeep of the road.

Apart from the turnpike the responsibility for the roads lay with the parishes. As a result, and through lack of funds, the roads were often in a sad state of disrepair. In 1861 when the parish of Harlow faced an indictment at the Quarter Sessions for not repairing the lanes in the north-east part of the parish, Mr Perry Watlington offered to give half the amount of gravel required. However, the Vestry declined this offer and decided to defend itself at the Quarter Sessions.

A subject which occupied the local authorities at the end of the nineteenth century is one which is relevant today. In 1895 the Parish Council was concerned about gypsy encampments on Harlow Common amounting to some twenty vans or more. A keeper was appointed in 1904 to prevent the gypsies from camping on common land. This did not always prove effective.

The 'Harlow Volunteer Fire Brigade' was formed in 1907, with Richard Hutchin acting as 'boss'. To call the Brigade together a fireman ran round the town ringing a hand bell. The uniform consisted of a black straight-rimmed hat and reefer jacket, similar to the uniform worn by man o' war's men. The Fire Station was situated near to the Green Man at Mulberry Green where it still stands. In 1895 the Fire Brigade was taken over by Harlow Parish Council, a new fire engine was purchased, and Sam Deards, a local business man, was confirmed as Captain. The following year new uniforms were provided at a cost of £21. Sam Deards served with the Fire Brigade for thirty-five years, being Captain for thirty years.

The clay soil of this area created a particular problem with regard to the disposal of sewage. Because of the soil, drainage was quite inadequate and often the Lee Conservancy Board had to complain to the Vestry about the pollution caused by lack of proper sewage disposal. As recently as 1861 two people died from typhus at Hobbs Cross and the local doctor complained that the drainage was bad. Although the Public Health Act of 1848 compelled local authorities to instal sewerage and appoint inspectors, the Vestries were reluctant to face the heavy expense involved. The problem was still with the authorities when Harlow Parish Council was formed, and instances even occurred during the early years of the Urban District Council when action had to be taken against property owners not having proper sanitation.

The Local Government Acts of 1888 and 1894 transferred most of the powers enjoyed by the Parish Council to the County Council and the Rural District Councils; the Essex County Council and the Epping Rural District Council managed the affairs of this area and its needs until 1955 when the present Harlow Urban District Council was formed.

It remains to say something about measures for home defence. From Saxon days each village had been liable to supply its complement for the local guard, and all through the medieval period the View of the Freeman had served as a muster and provided a list of those capable of bearing arms in each Hundred. A peculiar custom dating back to Saxon days was still kept in the Hundreds of Ongar, Waltham, and Harlow as late as the sixteenth century—the watch over the Ward-staff. Full details of this ceremony are preserved for the Ongar Hundred, and

may be found in Morant's *History of Essex*. About a fortnight after
Easter a draped staff, symbolizing the King, was set up at certain
stations in the Hundred where a barrier was erected across the road and
the local guard kept watch all night. When the various stations had
been kept the staff was passed on to the next Hundred, and so on until
it reached the coast by the Suffolk border, where it was cast into the
sea. The same practice was in force in the Half-hundreds of Waltham
and Harlow, but there is no record of the particular stations where the
watches were kept. A manor at Chingford was held by the service of
the Ward-staff in the thirteenth century, showing that the custom was
still preserved in the Waltham Half-hundred. At Latton the field on the
right-hand of the road from Harlow to Netteswell Cross just at the
boundary between Latton and Netteswell was called 'Ward-hatches';
here the barrier was set up on the night that watch was kept over the
Ward-staff.

There was a muster for home defence in Elizabeth I's reign when
the Spanish Armada was expected. Under James I a territorial force
was regularly equipped and periodically paraded; to this each Hundred was expected to supply 200 trained men, armed with pikes,
muskets or calivers, the latter being fire-arms lighter and more handy
than the long musket. Actually the Hundreds varied so much in size
and population that adjustments were made, and Harlow and Waltham
combined to provide one company; this was commanded in 1613 by
Sir Edward Altham and in 1622 by Richard Bugge. The territorials, or
trained bands, were called out in the civil war to support the Parliament.
There is extant a list of the horses, dragoons, and foot arms (infantry)
charged upon the Hundred of Harlow, August 15, 1659. Only the more
substantial inhabitants were taxed, less than twenty in (Old) Harlow,
where Mr Addington, Lord of Harlowbury, was charged to supply one
horse, seventeen householders to provide muskets, and one other to
furnish a pike. The two Parndons had to provide one dragoon, five
muskets, and a pike. Latton furnished a horse and four muskets;
Netteswell one horse, two muskets and one pike. By a statute of
Charles II the trophy tax was established; this enabled the Crown to
obtain money for the maintenance of the national militia. In 1696 Mr
Wooton notes in the Little Parndon register that the trophy money
came to £1 13s 6d a year at Great Parndon, and 12s a year at Little
Parndon. The threat of the Napoleonic invasion inspired a general call
to arms, and it was then that Montague Burgoyne raised his troop of
yeomanry. This volunteer troop was disbanded in 1828, but in 1830
the West Essex Yeomanry was formed and supported by this district,
and continued until 1877. When the Territorial Army came into being,
a local headquarters was established at Harlow with drill-hall and other

buildings. It stands in Old Road at no great distance from the mound which many centuries ago was the rallying-point for the local force and which has given Harlow its name.

Chapter 13
Harlow since 1947

The story of Harlow so far has been about a relatively quiet, rural area, having only slender links with London and the surrounding towns and villages. It has been the story of an agricultural population, with little trade and industry, with the church and squirearchy firmly at the head of a social structure within which everyone knew his or her place— a pattern of life which ended only a few decades before the coming of the new town. However, there is an interesting (though unintentional) early reference to a new town in this area. The historian Morant wrote in 1768 about the origin of the name 'Latton':

> '*The name ſeems to be formed from Late town,*
> *denoting a town or pariſh lately erected out*
> *of the Foreſt; meaning the ſame as New Town.*'

On the other hand Dr Reaney, in *The Place Names of Essex*, considers that it was probably derived from the Old English 'leactun', meaning kitchen-garden. Whether Morant was right or wrong, he may be said to have been 200 years ahead of his time.

New Towns—why and how

The profound changes which have occurred in Harlow since 1947 had several causes. During the war of 1939–45 house building throughout the country virtually stopped; thousands of homes were destroyed; immediately after the war the birth rate had risen sharply. At the same time many of our cities had become too big. Even while the war was in progress thought had been given to this vast problem, and one step in the process of solving it found expression in 'The New Towns Act' introduced in 1946 by the Rt Hon Lewis Silkin, MP, then Minister of Town and Country Planning, later to become Lord Silkin. A cluster of new towns was planned around London, of which Harlow was one of the first.

The machinery for planning and developing these new towns was achieved by setting up a separate Development Corporation for each of them, the Board Members being appointed by the Minister, and consisting of men and women who were prominent in the field of housing, local government, town planning and social welfare. Funds were advanced by the Treasury at prevailing rates of interest. It was recognized that no immediate return was possible, but it was hoped that a return would in due course be forthcoming as a result of commercial and industrial development.

The New Town of Harlow—early days

Before a decision could be taken to build a new town at Harlow, much preliminary thinking and planning had to take place. Mr Silkin appointed an Advisory Committee under the chairmanship of Sir Ernest Gowers, GBE, KCB. This Committee first met on October 9, 1946, and held thirteen meetings prior to the establishment of the Development Corporation. Mr Silkin also appointed Frederick Gibberd, FRIBA, (knighted in June 1967) to prepare a plan for the town to find out whether its construction on this particular site was feasible and what area of land would be required. Mr Gibberd first met the Advisory Committee on October 22, 1946. In due course a Designation Order was issued by the Minister specifying the site of the new town, and the establishment of the Development Corporation was authorized.

Harlow Development Corporation was formed on May 16, 1947, with Sir Ernest Gowers as its Chairman, W. Eric Adams, OBE, previously Town Clerk of Islington, as its General Manager, with the members of the former Advisory Committee becoming the first Members of the Corporation. The area allocated for development as a new town was 6,320 acres, with a population of approximately 4,500 and a rateable value of £26,509. It is interesting to note that in 1968 the rateable value of Harlow had grown to over £4,000,000 making it the fourth richest town in Essex and richer than many established towns throughout the country including Burnley, Hull, Grimsby and Gloucester.

The first act of the new Development Corporation was to appoint Mr Gibberd as the Architect Planner for Harlow. He prepared a Master Plan for creating out of the green fields, woods, hills and valleys a town which could house some 60,000 people from London. This target was later increased to 80,000 and subsequently, in 1967, to 90,000.

The designation of Harlow as a site for a new town inevitably caused some anxiety amongst those who felt that their land, property, business interests or ways of life might be affected, and the Members of the Corporation recognized that the task of winning local support for their plans might not be easy. They were only too well aware of the resistance encountered at Stevenage (the first new town to be designated) and the resulting serious delays. Some local residents felt that the coming of the new town would bring new industry, better jobs, new schools, shops and amenities. Others who had land or property interests were apprehensive and the Harlow and District Defence Association was formed. In order to give the local people as much information as possible the Corporation arranged an exhibition of the Master Plan from December 6–13, 1947, and nearly 3,000 people attended. This

XV *The Royal Visit, October 30, 1957*

XVI Town Hall and Water Gardens

succeeded in allaying most of the concern as to the Corporation's intentions and the Defence Association was subsequently wound up.

Amongst those most deeply affected were the landed proprietors whose farms, family mansions or estates would sooner or later be engulfed. They included William Soper of New Hall Farm who farmed extensively where the first development was to take place, the Arkwright family at Mark Hall and Parndon Hall, the Drakes and Todhunters whose families had long and close associations with the district.

Their acceptance of the situation helped to create a constructive atmosphere in which old and new could grow together. Mr Soper remained to play an important part as Chairman of the Joint Parishes Committee from its inception until 1952, and as a member of the Harlow Parish Council and a magistrate. The Joint Parishes Committee, representative of the then local authorities in the area, did much to smooth the introduction of the new town and gave the opportunity for the public to make their views known to the Corporation through their elected representatives, and for the Corporation to inform the public of its policy.

Brigadier Todhunter continued his outstanding service on the local Magistrates' Bench and to the service of youth through the local Scouts' Association. Colonel Drake, a collateral descendant of the famous Sir Francis Drake, stayed on to become one of the pioneers of music in the new town.

Others who welcomed the new town for the advantages they felt it would bring, accepted the challenge of change and prepared to play their parts in the new political framework which would inevitably emerge.

With the opposition virtually won over, the Corporation was able to deposit the Master Plan with the Minister for approval on January 12, 1948, and after a brief and uneventful public enquiry it received formal assent on March 15, 1949. The Minister, speaking in Victoria Hall, Old Harlow, in January 1948, said that 'Harlow does appear to be the only one of the new towns which has not gone to the Courts'.

Meanwhile a United Service of Dedication of the new town was held in Harlow Parish Church on October 3, 1948, attended by the Minister of Town and Country Planning and the Bishop of Chelmsford. Representatives of all the local authorities in the area and of over forty other organizations were present.

The Master Plan
Since many of the characteristics of Harlow, both physical and social, spring from the Master Plan, a brief description of it is essential to an

understanding of the development and history of modern Harlow. The Master Plan has the simple purpose of providing a framework for building development. Without a plan there would be chaos. But it can have a much deeper purpose—to give greater freedom to the individual than he would have without planning. The broad solution to the problem of planning a town consists of making a distinct separation between areas for work, homes and play, connected by a road pattern in which traffic can flow easily, and surrounded by a well-defined agricultural belt, but it must also achieve a balance between housing, varied work opportunities, and social amenities.

It is to the character of the landscape in which the town is to be built that the designer first looks in his search for individuality. This means using the form of the land itself, shaped thousands of years ago as described in Chapter 1. Only after the land had been walked over, its character learned, and its potential use studied, did the design begin to emerge. The shape of the land led to the idea of planning the housing and its services, such as shops, in four main groups on high ground leaving the natural valleys and streams between them. Through these broad sweeps of open countryside the main parkways run, with views of large building groups such as Netteswell Comprehensive School or the Town Centre from Second and Third Avenue. This broad flow of landscape in between the groups of buildings gives people a chance to walk and drive about the town in natural surroundings and prevents it congealing into one vast mass of buildings.

The main railway and river run in the Stort valley which forms the northern boundary of Harlow, with the main railway station near the midway point of the boundary, and the Town Centre lying to the south of it. Industry is situated in two major estates, east and west, connected by main roads to one another, to the railway and to the Town Centre. The reasons for planning two industrial estates were to get a better traffic distribution over the town than would be possible with only one estate, and to avoid having too large an industrial scene which might dominate the rest of the town and turn it virtually into two towns, one for living and one for working.

The houses were planned in four neighbourhood clusters, three around neighbourhood shopping centres (The Stow, Bush Fair, Staple Tye) and the fourth in association with the Town Centre. The old villages of Harlow and Potter Street were planned to form expanded neighbourhoods of their own. This pattern is illustrated in the diagram on page 131.

Near the centre of each of the big neighbourhood clusters is a main shopping area with more than thirty shops, services such as the branch Public Library, the Group Practice and Clinic Centre, the Com-

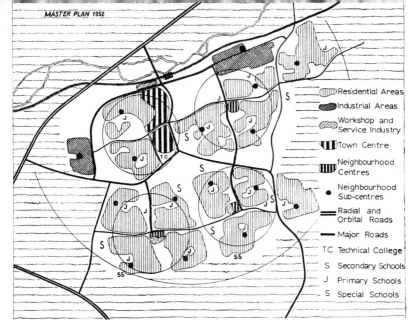

Fig. 10. The Master Design. Four clusters set in a broad landscape pattern: Old Harlow and Potter Street are appendages to the east. (Note: it is now proposed that the Motorway should be moved from the north boundary to the east)

Fig. 11. Neighbourhood Pattern (Bush Fair). Three neighbourhoods each with a primary school and sub-shopping centre as its focus, grouped to form one large Neighbourhood Cluster with a major shopping and social centre

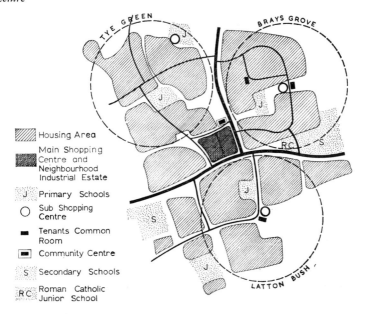

munity Centre, and an area of service industry while at Bush Fair and Staple Tye there are areas of light manufacturing industry.

Within each of the four neighbourhood clusters, there is a series of neighbourhoods. The diagram on page 131 shows the Bush Fair neighbourhood cluster, surrounded by its component neighbourhoods of Brays Grove, Latton Bush and Tye Green. Each neighbourhood has a primary school at the centre so that few children have to cross main roads to go to and from school. Adjacent to the school is a small sub-centre (or 'Hatch') comprising a small group of 'round-the-corner' shops, a public house, a meeting hall and sometimes a church.

Within each neighbourhood is another group—the housing area such as Orchard Croft or Shawbridge, each area designed by a different architect, to give variety of architectural design, and to give people a sense of belonging to a place of recognizable character. The focus of the town's corporate activities is 'The High', the town centre, sited by the Master Plan on a high plateau originally known as Dad's Wood, in the heart of the designated area. 'The High' acts not only as the principal shopping, commercial and civic centre, but also the main centre for further education through the Technical College, and for leisure activities through the bowling alley, cinema, sportcentre, Town Park with swimming pool and other amusements, restaurants, and—in due time—a theatre. The plan from the outset provided that the Centre itself should be traffic-free: it consists of a series of pedestrian walks and squares from which traffic is excluded. Because of the heavy impact on towns of the motor car, the shopping area of the Town Centre is surrounded by car parks, and (as a modification to the original Master Plan) most of these are to be replaced by multi-storey car parks connected by bridges to the shopping area. When first mooted the idea of turning a town centre inside-out and placing buildings away from the roads, was so unusual that it met considerable opposition. But experience has shown that the idea was sound.

The initial task of implementing the Master Plan was accompanied by considerable frustration. Both money and man-power were short. The Government therefore decided that work should, in general, be limited during 1948 to starting upon civil engineering works to provide roads, water supplies and drainage, and should use in all not more than an average of 300 workers.

Harlow had special difficulties to contend with at the outset, since the existing services of water supply and drainage were hopelessly inadequate for a town of 80,000. In fact the Corporation's Engineers had to survey the hills and valleys of Hertfordshire seeking adequate sources of water; also miles of sewers had to be laid, and an entirely new road system created. On the other hand this lack of facilities represented a great advantage for the designers. They started with 'a clean sheet' and were able to plan the new town without having to compromise with an existing town structure.

Early Housing and Industrial Development

When a start could be made on housing it necessarily had to be in, or near, Old Harlow, where essential shops and services (a main road and a railway station) already existed. Thus the first houses began to rise on a site in the old town, and on August 4, 1949, the first two tenants received their keys. By December of that year, tenants had begun to move in to Chippingfield (the area where a medieval market had been held). But the days of economic stringency were not over, and the early post-war years involved a constant battle to get money, labour and materials.

This was not the only battle which had to be fought: houses were going up but no factories to provide employment for the tenants because building licences could not be obtained. Moreover the whole process of developing the town was being hindered by multiplication of controls. The Annual Report of Harlow Development Corporation for the year 1949/50 stated 'The Harlow Corporation would be . . . disposed to say that they (the multiplicity of controls) create machinery which is in some respects cumbrous almost past belief and which produces in profusion officials doing one after another work that one official could well have been trusted to do by himself. Development Corporations have too many masters'.

In the Report for the following year it was possible to express gratitude for the impetus given to industrial development by the personal intervention of the Minister. It was at this time that Sir Ernest Gowers relinquished the Chairmanship of the Corporation, being replaced by Richard (later Sir Richard) Costain, CBE, FIOB. During the year in question twelve industrial undertakings had been enabled to move to Harlow, and a major problem had been solved. The Corporation during subsequent years maintained a policy of establishing a diversified industrial structure, to avoid undue dependence on a single industry. Once the initial break-through had been achieved with the easing of building restrictions there was no serious difficulty in attracting industry to Harlow, and in securing suitable types of industry—light engineering, electronics, research laboratories, glassworks, food manufacture, and many similar light industries. In November 1952 the Temple Fields Industrial Estate was visited by HRH The Duke of Edinburgh, who gave his name to Edinburgh Way.

Shops, Schools and Social Provision

In the early days employment was not the only problem to be faced. In step with the building of houses and factories had to come the development of new shopping areas, new schools and other social provision which would serve residents as the town began to extend away from Old Harlow towards the south and west.

The development of shops, industry and commercial amenities has had to be a co-ordinated process throughout the life of the town. Shop-keepers cannot be expected to come to a town until there are sufficient residents to guarantee sales. On the other hand residents expect to find shops when they arrive. Similarly, proprietors of entertainment facilities will not incur heavy expenditure until adequate audiences can be expected—but long before then the residents will feel the need for such facilities. Moreover, in early days residents feared that their children would be deprived of proper education.

The first problem—shopping—was partly overcome by relating new buildings to an existing village or hamlet—Old Harlow and Potter Street, where some shops existed which could meet the initial need, while others were being built in the neighbourhood centres and 'Hatches'. The need for entertainment was met by the acquisition in October 1952 of the old St Mary-at-Latton vicarage for use as a com-munity centre (Moot House), by the construction of tenants' com-mon rooms for use by residents and local organizations, and by the adaptation of an empty factory building to serve as a temporary cinema, The Regal, which was opened in August 1952. Farm fields were used for football and cricket, and a shallow disused gravel pit was developed as a children's playground. The first Health Centre—Haygarth House in Mark Hall North—was simply two houses adapted to meet this need. The keynote of those early days for entertainment, activities and general social amenities was improvisation: a little help from the authorities was supplemented by much initiative on the part of local residents. At the same time church halls were being built to supplement the work of the ancient churches existing in the town and the first new town public house—'The Essex Skipper', was opened in The Stow in 1952. Alongside all these activities the need for sculpture and other works of art was not overlooked, and the town was able to acquire first 'Contrapuntal Forms' by Barbara Hepworth (sited in Glebelands) and the promise of contributions to justify the formation of the Harlow Art Trust.

Limitations on capital expenditure threatened to slow up the pro-vision of schools to meet the needs of the incoming population, the majority of whom were families with young children. As the result of urgent representations by the Corporation and the Education Authority a number of school projects were approved. In April 1952 children who had been temporarily housed in the old Mark Hall Mansion were able to move to the new Tanys Dell Primary School. Work on the Mark Hall Secondary School had been started and it came partially into use in 1953. This school was conveniently situated to serve the growing Old Harlow area, and the new areas being built round The Stow.

Some Problems of Housing Policy

From the outset each housing area was planned for a balanced community, to comprise dwellings—houses and flats—designed for all income groups and differing family sizes. The architects in planning the housing areas endeavoured to avoid uniform rows of two-storey dwellings all looking alike, and of creating instead areas with character and identity of their own. Green landscaped spaces were provided in or adjacent to each housing area.

In February 1950 Mr Gibberd designed one of the first residential tower blocks in this country—'The Lawn', sited in the north-west corner between First Avenue and the new A.11. The tower was opened by The Rt Hon Hugh Dalton on May 9, 1951, and it received a Festival of Britain award for architecture.

Initially, residents had to rent their dwellings: it was not until 1957 that the first area of houses for sale—Upper Park—was completed by the Corporation, though at the same time private developers were constructing houses for sale in the town. With the passage of the years both government policy and social policy underwent changes. More houses were built for sale: similarly the small area of mixed social structure gave place to larger areas. This latter change was partly to secure the economic advantages of building larger blocks of similar dwellings, but also showed an awareness that proximity had not created social mixing between different classes in the community. Despite these changes, Harlow appears to have been successful in avoiding an 'East End' and a 'West End'.

In 1953/54 housing development—and the related amenities—was progressing in the Potter Street, Tye Green, Hare Street and Little Parndon neighbourhoods. The main A.11 (London Road) had not yet been diverted to its present course according to the Master Plan, and thus heavy traffic continued to flow through Potter Street, as in the old days of the stage coaches whose journeys are referred to in Chapter 10. Nowadays the cars, lorries and through coaches speed along the diverted main road clear of built-up areas as intended. However, the old Potter Street village had a nucleus of shops, and social and recreational facilities, and it was possible to extend or adapt these to meet the needs of a larger community.

One of those who helped to bridge the gulf between the old Potter Street and the new was Jack Stevens, a retired London policeman locally known as 'The Mayor of Potter Street'. Right up to his death in 1967 Mr Stevens continued to play a notable part not only in Potter Street but in the wider affairs of the new town. William Fisher of Netteswell is another pre-new town resident who has well served the Council, the Corporation and the town.

The Town Centre
Meanwhile work had been progressing on detailed plans for the Town Centre. Many authorities were consulted before its submission to the Minister in March 1952. The first area to be developed was the Market Square in the north, whose surrounding shops were to act as a neighbourhood shopping centre for Hare Street and Little Parndon residents. The commemoration stone in the Market Square, in the middle of a wind-swept plateau, was unveiled on May 21, 1955, by The Rt Hon Duncan Sandys, then Minister of Housing and Local Government. Just before Christmas of the same year the first Town Centre traders opened their shops in Market Square, and the Market itself was opened on Whit Saturday, May 19, 1956, by Alderman T. H. Joyce, Deputy Chairman of the Corporation.

Later, the Town Centre became a focal point for large stores, and for the establishment in the town of commercial offices, large and small. These served two purposes: they gave the town needed services—solicitors, insurance offices, government offices, etc., but also provided employment for school-leavers seeking clerical or secretarial work. As larger offices came to Harlow, such as Joseph Rank, British Petroleum, Gilbeys and Longmans Green, those opportunities for employment were greatly expanded.

The pace quickens and new ideas are introduced
By March 1954, the 4,000th dwelling to be built by the Corporation had been completed. The population had grown from 4,500 to 17,000 in a period of four to five years. In the years immediately following, the rate of expansion accelerated not only in the building of houses, but in factories, offices, schools, shops, churches, community centres and tenants' common rooms, and the many amenities required for residents.

This acceleration in the momentum of development owed much to the leadership of the Corporation's Chairman, Sir Richard Costain, with his experience as head of a great international building and civil engineering firm, and the dynamic energy of Eric Adams, the first General Manager. In 1955 Mr Adams resigned and was succeeded by B. Hyde Harvey, formerly Comptroller and Chief Finance Officer of the Corporation, who has continued to the present time. In 1968 he was awarded the OBE for his distinguished services to the town.

As time went by, new ideas and new constructional methods were applied to housing. In Latton Bush some of the housing areas were designed on the Radburn principle, the dwellings being planned around rear garage and service courts, with the houses fronting mainly on to pedestrian ways. Central heating came more and more to be recognized as essential. Provision was made in areas to be built in the 1960s for a garage for every car, together with hardstanding provision for visitors' cars and for the 'second' car. New materials and methods were used for houses, facilitating faster construction. In 1965 and 1966 housing areas were built (Old Orchard, Bishopsfield and Charters Cross) as prize-winning schemes resulting from competitions. All areas were land-scaped, so that in course of time the appearance of the town became mellowed by trees, shrubberies and rose beds.

Harlow Urban District Council

From its inception the Development Corporation was having to fulfil many of the functions of a local authority because, in what had been a rural area, there was no large-scale authority able to provide the amenities needed by a rapidly-expanding town. Close contact had been maintained with Essex County Council for the provision of schools, for the amenities required by young people and by adults, for health, welfare and police services. But the formation of the Harlow Urban District Council on April 1, 1955, enabled the normal functions of local government to be carried out by the town's own elected body. By this time the population was well over 20,000.

At the first elections in May 1955 eighteen Councillors were elected, five from the old communities and thirteen representing the newer parts of the town. Their first Chairman was Alfred Brown, born and bred in the district and one of the stalwarts of the local Labour Party. The grant of the Coat of Arms to the Council was made by Lord Silkin on October 26, 1957, in the Market Square.

Until the first Clerk of the Council could be appointed the Engineer and Surveyor, A. W. R. Webb, continued to act, but in September 1955 Douglas Bull, former Deputy Town Clerk of Luton, was appointed Clerk to the newly established Urban District Council.

During the first five years of its existence the Council had to under-take a succession of important capital projects as the population con-tinued to increase; the development of many public playing fields, the swimming pool opened for use in the summer of 1961, the provision of a crematorium and burial ground and the building of the Municipal Offices and Town Hall opened on July 9, 1960, by Earl Attlee. The second stage of the Town Hall—a nine-storey office block designed by Frederick Gibberd with an observation room on the roof—was completed in November 1963. Fountains, pools and formal water gardens make an impressive setting for the civic buildings which dominate the Town Centre.

Great progress has been made by the Council in the development of the Town Park, stretching from First Avenue to the River Stort in the north and covering 240 acres. Broad landscape areas provide for family open air recreation, and there is an attractive modern cafe and club room at 'Spurriers' with an open-air dance floor and skating rink. Its eight-acre grounds include specimen and water gardens and a special Pets' Corner which has proved a great attraction for the children. The Council has also opened two paddling pools in the Town Park near the main swimming pool, climbing playgrounds and a road safety training ground.

The Council has taken very seriously its responsibilities as Museum Authority under the Public Libraries and Museums Act 1964. A Museum Workshop was established in the Town Park in 1968 and contains documents and 'finds' relating to this area. Items of special interest in the Workshop are glassware, pottery, clay pipes and coins of Venetian, German, Dutch and local origin dating back to the sixteenth and seventeenth centuries, discovered in 1960 when the old well of Mark Hall Mansion was investigated. The Council has also pursued a policy of providing public entertainment for all ages, aid to the elderly, and support for voluntary organizations, especially in the field of sport and the arts.

All these amenity services have had to be provided by the Council at a time of extremely high building and development costs, and they have inevitably posed a challenge and a heavy financial burden.

A sign of Harlow's increasing maturity was seen in its desire to form links of friendship with a town of similar size overseas. Eventually the Council arranged that Harlow's 'twin town' should be Stavanger, a 900-year-old town in Norway, and in September 1960 the Mayor and Clerk of Stavanger, with their wives, were invited on an official civic visit to Harlow to mark the inauguration of the scheme. As a result, many exchanges have been made between individuals, school parties and organizations in the two towns. Unfortunately, in April 1962 the Chairman of the Urban District Council, Councillor Marriott and Mrs Marriott were tragically killed in a car crash while on an official visit to Stavanger.

From the outset there was close co-operation between the Corporation and the Council with specific machinery for joint consultation. Considerable difficulties have arisen from time to time, and there have been very real differences of opinion, but with goodwill on both sides these have generally been resolved.

Co-operation has been facilitated by the appointment of local Councillors to the Board of the Corporation by the Minister. Prior to the formation of the Urban District Council the Minister had no option but to appoint to the Board specialist representation from outside the town.

A new Chairman of the Development Corporation

In July 1966 the distinguished educationist, Sir John Newsom, CBE, LLD, famed for the Newsom Report 'Half Our Future', but also prominently connected with one of Harlow's leading firms, was appointed as Chairman of the Corporation following the death of Sir Richard Costain in March of that year.

Police

With the building of the Police Station in the Town Centre in 1957 Harlow became a Police Division of Essex County Constabulary. In the earlier days the Harlow Magistrates' Court was held in a small building behind the old police headquarters in Old Harlow, but the growing size of the town made it necessary to provide a bigger and more central building for the Magistrates' Courts and in September 1959 the Lord Lieutenant of Essex, Sir John Ruggles-Brise, CB, OBE, TD, JP, opened the new court-house, which also housed the first County Court from February 1961.

Health Services

A feature of modern Harlow has been the development of unusual facilities for the health services. In 1950 the Essex County Council through its Medical Officer of Health Dr Kenneth Cowan (knighted in 1958) prepared schemes for Health Centres in Harlow, initially at a cost of £80,000, later modified to £40,000, but both schemes were rejected by the Ministry. The cause was however taken up with immense vigour by Dr Stephen Taylor (later Lord Taylor of Harlow) a member of the Harlow Development Corporation Board, who was engaged on research into general medical practice for the Nuffield Provincial Hospitals Trust. As a result the Nuffield Trust in 1952 made a generous grant for the establishment of a temporary Health Centre in Mark Hall North for medical and dental services and Local Health Authority Clinics. This, as already mentioned, was housed in improvised accommodation. It was named Haygarth House and visited by the Rt Hon Harold Macmillan, then Minister of Housing and Local Government.

The Trust later provided the capital to build three permanent centres to serve the Potter Street, Mark Hall and Netteswell neighbourhoods, and these were officially opened in October 1955 by Lord Nuffield himself. Another centre was built in 1957 to serve local needs in Little Parndon and Hare Street, and this centre housed additional services such as a Child Guidance Clinic, Orthopaedic and Orthoptic clinic, and an X-ray Unit for the whole town. By 1967 there were six Group Practice and Clinic Centres serving all parts of the town, apart from the original village of Old Harlow where space was reserved for a seventh centre in the plans for re-development of the High Street.

During 1955 another unique venture in British medicine was started in Harlow with the launching of the Harlow Industrial Health Service, designed to give twenty-four-hour cover for accidents and illnesses occurring at work, first aid training and specialist advice to firms engaged on processes with potential health hazards. The Nuffield Provincial Hospitals Trust provided the capital for research on the scheme, and then for building and equipping the premises, with member firms contributing to the cost of running the service, and local family doctors and industrial nursing sisters providing the medical care. The drive in initiating this venture also came from Dr Stephen Taylor.

The first centre at Edinburgh House in Temple Fields was officially opened in 1957, and in 1960 a smaller centre was opened on the western industrial estate. A similar but smaller centre served the Bush Fair industrial area from November 1965. This pioneer industrial health venture which is outside the National Health Service has continued to attract many visitors from home and abroad.

Hopes for a hospital in Harlow were slow in coming to fruition. Provision had been made for a site, and plans were being prepared as early as 1951. The slow rate of progress in the provision of a hospital gave rise to considerable local concern, and indeed to much criticism. Eventually the first stage of the building, for out-patient care, was opened in 1961, and the Princess Alexandra Hospital was officially opened by Princess Alexandra in 1965, but it was not until May 1967 that the 323-bed hospital was fully completed.

Meanwhile there was an important administrative change in 1962 with the creation by Essex County Council of the Harlow Health Area and the appointment of the Medical Officer of Health as Area Medical Officer and Divisional School Medical Officer.

Community Activities

The growth of social, cultural, community and sporting amenities was an equal partnership between residents and the local authorities. The community centres and tenants' common rooms, for example, although provided initially by the Corporation, (the community centres later being maintained by the Local Education Authority), were entirely dependent on the residents so far as activities were concerned. The high reputation enjoyed by the town for its cultural life sprang from the readiness of residents to form drama groups, vocal and orchestral groups for all ages, and led to the formation of the Harlow Music Association in 1957 and the Harlow Arts Council in 1964, assisted by grants from the local authorities, but with energy, drive and talent provided by people living in the town.

The Harlow Art Trust to which reference has already been made is an entirely independent body which has been supported by industrialists and residents in the town and which has bequeathed to Harlow a remarkably fine collection of sculptures in varying traditions, which are sited throughout the town. The expert advice of Sir Philip Hendy, formerly Director of the National Gallery, and of Henry Moore (whose work is represented in the town), has materially assisted the acquisition of suitable sculpture, and a few paintings which are on show in buildings accessible to the public.

As an aid to social and cultural activities, the Corporation built Stone Cross Hall in the Town Centre, opened in 1956 and designed for multi-purpose use—dances, concerts, dinners, exhibitions, drama and ballet. The hall had to be subsidized by the Corporation, but for many years it served a valuable purpose as a centre for many activities.

Once the Music Association and the Arts Council were formed, a forum was provided for still further expansion of cultural activities. The visit to Netteswell School of the London Philharmonic Orchestra under its conductor Sir Adrian Boult drew a capacity audience; since then the Arts Council has launched the annual Harlow Arts Festival, supported financially by the Urban District Council and first held in 1965. This brings together both amateur talent, and artists of international repute. Harlow was the first town in England to sponsor its own resident professional chamber music ensemble, the Alberni String Quartet, who gave their first concert in 1963. A grant by the Calouste Gulbenkian Foundation made possible the establishment of this group, which is now assisted financially by the Urban District Council. The Quartet gives regular concerts in the town and is winning a high repute nationally and internationally. The growth of drama and ballet, the encouragement of music and the arts in the schools of Harlow, the many fine sculptures in the town, and the development of the town as a 'going concern', are vividly reflected in the film about Harlow made for the Corporation in 1963. The premiere of 'Faces of Harlow' was held at the Odeon Cinema on November 30, 1964, and was followed in January 1965 by another film, 'The Pied Pipers of Harlow', illustrating the wide range of musical activity in the town. A showing on BBC television attracted national attention to this portrayal of local talent.

The Central Library and its branches, in addition to the issue of books and gramophone records, has made a valuable contribution to the cultural and artistic life of the town and its environs. The Central Library's stock of 90,000 books attracts readers from a wide area outside Harlow. Since 1963 it has mounted more than fifty exhibitions including regular shows by local artists and photographers and displays of Arts Council reproductions. In addition the library provides a quiet study area for students, and meeting rooms for local societies.

The Harlow Urban District Council has been working actively for the establishment of the town's Theatre and Arts Centre to include a regional film theatre, gallery space, workshops, lounge bars, club rooms, rehearsal rooms, and a completely adaptable 500-seat auditorium. The total cost of the building will be about £430,000. However, at least £100,000 has been promised by Harlow Development Corporation and the Arts Council of Great Britain has promised a further £47,500. Essex County Council will donate £5,000 and the British Film Institute equipment worth about £8,000 and maintenance support. The balance will be provided by the Urban District Council. Responsibility for the management, programme and development of the theatre is vested in the Harlow Theatre Trust established in 1965 and representing all the interests involved.

A similar story of amenities being actively developed by residents for residents applies to sport. The Harlow and District Sports Trust was formed in 1958 with the aim of providing a centre with first class opportunities for every major sport. With generous grants from many local and national bodies, and with financial support from local residents, the Sportcentre adjacent to the Town Centre was progressively developed between 1958 and 1964, in which year the large three-storey Sports Hall was completed—though in 1968 further extensions began.

It was in 1964 that the eighteen-hole golf course was completed and an old farm building converted into a luxurious modern Club House. The course, leased to the Harlow and District Sports Trust and designed by Henry Cotton, was officially opened in May 1966.

These developments were a measure of the growing stature of the town. From the outset ample provision had been made for playing fields and tennis courts, initially by improvisation and later by planned development. These were in due course taken over and expanded by the Urban District Council and are well patronized by many football, rugby, hockey, cricket and tennis clubs. The Harlow Sports Council was established in 1964 to co-ordinate all sporting activities.

Throughout the life of the new town, the population pattern has been of special interest to the planners, and has had a marked effect on the development of the town. The early settlers were characteristically young couples. Older people were in general less willing to face the rigours of the early days—mud, the general debris of building, shortage of the amenities that are taken for granted in an established town, distance from shops. The youthfulness of the first new town residents gave rise to a high birth rate. Harlow at one time was known as a 'pram town'. This in turn led to the need for early primary school provision. As the town expanded, so more primary and secondary schools were built by Essex County Council, some being temporary schools to meet the requirements of a 'bulge' which would pass as the age range of the population became more balanced. Secondary education was organized initially through Bilateral Schools, though these were later made Comprehensive. Special provision was made for children having physical or mental handicaps. The College of Further Education (now termed the Harlow Technical College) opened its doors to students in 1958. Such has been the demand for places that further phases of expansion of the College have been necessary. In 1962 the Essex County Council formed a separate Education Division for Harlow, with headquarters in the Town Hall.

While the town was growing—in terms both of buildings and the average age of the population—the need to make provision for young people's activities was anticipated. The primary responsibility for youth provision rested on the Local Education Authority, but this was supplemented by voluntary and commercial services. Schools were extensively used as youth centres with support and financial backing from the Local Education Authority. The YWCA built the Galaxy Club, a purpose-built centre for youth activities. The churches, and, in particular the Scouts and Guides and other uniformed organizations, made provision for young people. The YMCA and YWCA jointly pioneered a children's play scheme, later taken over and greatly expanded by the Urban District Council. The Odeon Cinema, opened in 1960, and the ten-pin Bowling Centre, opened in 1962, provided informal recreation. In 1967 the Urban District Council took over Stone Cross Hall, renamed it 'The Birdcage', and converted it to become an up-to-date entertainment centre for Harlow and the surrounding district.

Another feature of interest to young people was the building by the YWCA of the Alexandra Residential Club, opened in 1969 and providing accommodation for 108 young men and women, with ancillary recreational facilities. This provides living accommodation for students and for young people whose homes are elsewhere.

As the years have gone by, the population structure has become more balanced; residents have brought their parents to live in the town;

young 'second generation' couples have been housed in dwellings of their own. By 1973 it is expected that the imbalances in age structure will have been practically eliminated for all ages up to sixty. Above this age however it will probably be another fifteen years before Harlow's population matches the rest of the country. Meanwhile the needs of old people have not been overlooked, and provision for them is made by the Urban District Council especially through their housing facilities for old people.

The old churches of the town have been described in Chapter 11, but the growth of the town created new needs which were met by the building of new churches, the first being St Andrew's Methodist church in The Stow opened in 1954. This was a dual purpose building, i.e. a combined church and church hall giving more economic use of space. By this time negotiations were in progress with other denominations—Church of England, Roman Catholic, Baptist, Congregational, Presbyterian, Salvation Army, Society of Friends and the Jewish faith, for the development of sites for their places of worship. In the meantime a number of these groups used tenants' common rooms and community centres for their worship. The new church of St Paul in the Town Centre was opened for worship in January 1959, and is notable for a striking mural in mosaic by John Piper. The following year saw the opening of the Roman Catholic Church of Our Lady of Fatima, for which the brilliant stained glass windows were designed and made by the monks of Buckfast Abbey. In an entirely different tradition is the simple austerity of the Evangelical Lutheran Church of the Redeemer in the heart of Bush Fair, which was dedicated on March 18, 1967. This church is notable for its flexibility of design and ingenious use of space.

As the years have gone by more and more voluntary organizations, covering well-nigh every aspect of social life, have grown up, to a total of nearly 500. Some of these organizations are supported by grants or through the provision of accommodation by the Urban District Council, the Development Corporation, Essex County Council and other statutory bodies. These widespread activities are a symptom of the vitality which is so characteristic of the town and they provide outlets for a very wide range of interests. The architects and planners could provide the 'body'—but the spirit of the town springs from the thousands of people who have made their home in it.

Harlow as 'news'

As the modern town of Harlow took shape, its new concepts of housing, town planning and community development made a strong impact not only on the rest of the country but also on specialist groups all over the world. Harlow was 'news'. It was given press, radio and television coverage at frequent intervals. It was visited by Royalty, Presidents, Prime Ministers and by other Senior Ministers, by individuals and groups from all parts of the world, usually with a special interest in one or other aspect of town planning; they came to see what was being done in Harlow and to take ideas back to their own countries. This flow of official visitors—some three to four thousand per year—still continues.

The most notable visit of all was on October 30, 1957, when Her Majesty The Queen and His Royal Highness Prince Philip, Duke of Edinburgh, came to Harlow. At Hugh's Tower the Queen was welcomed by the Lord Lieutenant of Essex and the Minister of Housing and Local Government. A two-hour tour included a panoramic description of the town from the top of Hugh's Tower, a visit to Mark Hall Secondary School and to the Harlow Metal Company's factory in Temple Fields, and the opening of Elizabeth Way (the new road built to link the two industrial estates).

Expansion Plan
Faced with the continuing attraction of population into the South East Region the Minister of Housing and Local Government in 1962 initiated feasibility studies into the possibility of expanding several towns in the area, Harlow being one of them. In 1963 an expansion survey involving a proposed extension to the boundaries of the town was drawn up and submitted to the Minister. The survey envisaged a growth to a planned ultimate figure of between 120,000 and 130,000 people. In November 1964 the Minister asked local authorities and other bodies for their observations on the scheme, but the Ministerial decision was delayed by considerations of regional planning, by delay in deciding on the site of London's third airport and by other problems.

In 1967, however, the Minister did inform the Corporation that he was satisfied that a population of 90,000 could be contained within the original Designated Area.

The advocates of expansion of Harlow along the lines proposed in 1963 argued that it would not only strengthen the industrial structure and the existing amenities of the town—in terms of money and participation by residents—but would also offer a better balance of employment and enable new facilities and larger shops to be provided.

Conclusion
From the outset the development of the new town of Harlow has been a co-operative task, initially between the Corporation's own architects and planners and then as the population has grown, increasingly

between the residents of Harlow, the Urban District Council, and the Corporation. The residents of the town owe a great debt to the planners of the late 1940s, but equally it must now give the planners immense satisfaction to look at the richly varied life of the people of Harlow.

Meanwhile it is clear that this quiet corner of Essex has seen more changes in the past twenty-one years than in the previous 2,000 years. The rural scene described in earlier chapters has given place to a prosperous town, providing home, work and leisure opportunities for many thousands of people, most of whom are newcomers to this area. Future historians may well conclude that more history has been made in Harlow since 1947 than in the whole of previous recorded time: it is the people of Harlow who are making it.

Appendix A
Members of the Board of Harlow Development Corporation

FOUNDER MEMBERS

Sir Ernest Gowers, GBE, KCB, *Chairman*	1947–1950
Major-General R. P. Pakenham-Walsh, CB, MC, *Deputy-Chairman*	1947–1950
B. G. K. Allsop, MC, JP	1947–1950
R. O. C. Hurst, FCS, JP, *Deputy-Chairman* 1950–1954	1947–1954
T. H. Joyce, *Deputy-Chairman* 1954–1961	1947–1963
Mrs E. A. Newton, BA, JP	1947–1952
A. Reed, JP	1947–1952
The Countess Russell	1947–1950
D. H. Whinney, MA(OXON)	1947–1949

SUBSEQUENT MEMBERS

R. R. Costain (later Sir Richard Costain), CBE, FIOB, *Chairman*	1950–1966
R. G. Leach, CBE, FCA	1950–1966
Dr S. J. L. Taylor (later Lord Taylor of Harlow), BSC, MD, MRCP	1950–1964 1966–1967
R. B. Williams-Thompson	1950–1952
F. A. Coates	1952–1956
J. P. Brown, BSC	1956–1963
Dame Alix Meynell, DBE	1956–1965
L. E. Norton, *Deputy-Chairman from* 1961	1957–
J. H. Newsom (later Sir John Newsom), CBE, LLD, *Chairman from* 1966	1961–
W. Fisher, JP	1961–1967

D. L. Anderson, TD, FLAS	1965–1967
R. S. Roberts	1965–
Dr H. B. O. Cardew, LMSSA	1965–
Lord Mitchison, CBE, QC	1966–
Mrs B. K. Lowton, JP	1967–
M. Lawn, MSC	1968–
A. Hardy, MA	1968–

Appendix B

Principal Officers of Harlow Development Corporation of long standing

General Manager	W. Eric Adams, CBE	1947–1955
	B. Hyde Harvey, OBE	1955–
Architect Planner	Sir Frederick Gibberd, CBE	1947–
Chief Architect	N. Tweddell	1947–1949
Executive Architect	V. Hamnett, BSC	1949–
Chief Engineer	O. W. Gilmour, MA	1947–1966
	B. E. Lewis, BSC	1966–1968
Chief Finance Officer	B. Hyde Harvey	1947–1955
	G. D. Bratt	1955–
Chief Solicitor	J. R. Jacques	1947–
Chief Estates Officer	R. D. Relf	1947–1952
Housing Manager	C. A. Jackman	1952–
Social Development Officer	Miss M. Green	1947–1950
Liaison Officer	L. E. White	1951–
Administrative Officer	Mrs J. Morgan	1947–
Commercial Estates Officer	L. Austin Crowe	1955–1962
	R. A. Childs	1962–

Appendix C

Chairmen of Harlow Urban District Council

A. E. Brown	1955–1956
G. L. Easteal, JP	1956–1957
D. L. Anderson, TD, FLAS	1957–1958
W. Fisher, JP	1958–1959
E. W. Buckle	1959–1960
J. H. Harris	1960–1961
G. B. Marriott	1961–1962
R. W. Dallas, JP, MA	1962–1963
R. J. Ward, JP	1963–1964
Mrs S. Anderson, BA	1964–1965
J. J. Davidson	1965–1966
R. S. Roberts	1966–1967
W. G. Arnott	1967–1968
D. R. Score, BA	1968–1969

Glossary

Advowson – right of presentation to a benefice.

Aisle – division of church, especially one parallel to and divided by pillars from the main nave, choir or transept.

Apsidal – of the form of an apse (semicircular or polygonal recess, arched or dome-roofed).

Attainder, Bill of – one introduced or passed in the English Parliament (first in 1459) for attaining (convicting) any one without a judicial trial.

Beadle – parish officer appointed by Vestry.

Bede-roll – a list of persons to be specially prayed for.

Benefice – church living: property held by an ecclesiastical officer, especially rector or vicar.

Cartulary – collection of records; register.

Cella – the body of the temple, as distinct from the portico or other external structures.

Chancel – eastern part of church reserved for clergy, choir, etc., and usually railed off.

Chantry – endowment for priest(s) to sing masses for founder's soul; priests, chapel, altar so endowed.

Chapel-of-ease – chapel for convenience of remote parishioners.

Choir – chancel of cathedral, minster or large church.

Circa (abbreviation c.) – about.

Clap-gate – a small door or gate which shuts when slammed, or which swings to of itself.

Clerestory – part of wall of cathedral or large church, with series of windows, above aisle roofs.

Cloister-garth – the open court enclosed by a cloister.

Copyhold – a kind of tenure in England of ancient origin: tenure of lands being parcel of a manor, 'at the will of the lord according to the custom of the manor', by copy of the manorial court-roll.

Crossing (N) – that part of a cruciform church where the transepts cross the nave.

Cruciform – cross-shaped.

Cupola – small rounded dome forming roof.

Cure (N) – the spiritual charge or oversight of parishioners or lay people.

Demesne – all of an owner's land not held of him by freehold tenants, or all that he actually occupies himself.

Episcopacy – government of church by bishops.

Escheat – lapsing of property to crown or lord of manor on owner's dying intestate without heirs.

Examinat – a person under examination, either as a witness or accused person.

Extent – (law) valuation (of land, etc.).

Fee – inherited estate.

Font – receptacle for baptismal water.

Heriot – render of best live beast or dead chattel, or money payment, to lord (of manor) on decease of tenant.

Incumbent – holder of ecclesiastical benefice.

Indenture – any sealed agreement or contract.

Inquisition – search, investigation; judicial or official enquiry.

Kilderkin – cask for liquids containing 16 or 18 gallons.

Living (N) – ecclesiastical benefice.

Mainprise – the action of making oneself legally responsible for the fulfilment of a contract or undertaking by another person; suretyship.

Messuage – dwelling house with outbuildings and land assigned to its use.

Moiety – half, especially in legal use; (loosely) one of two parts into which thing is divided.

Nave – body of church from west door to chancel, usually separated by pillars from aisles.

Oligarchy – government by the few; members of such government

Osseous – consisting of bone.

*Ox-bow lake – a lake formed when a meandering river, having bent in an almost complete circle, cuts across the narrow neck of land between the two stretches and leaves a backwater; silt is gradually deposited by the river at the entrances to this backwater, till the latter is finally separated from the river and becomes a lake.

Piscina – perforated stone basin in church for carrying away water used in rinsing chalice, etc.

Plurality of livings (pluralist) – holding of two or more benefices.

Portico – colonnade, roof supported by columns at regular intervals, usually attached as porch to a building.

Potsherd – broken piece of earthenware

Presbyterian – a church governed by elders, all (including ministers) of equal rank.

Present (V) – bring formally under notice, submit (complaint, offence, to authority).

Quit-rent – (usually small) rent paid by freeholder or copyholder in lieu of service.

Quoin (quoining) – external angle of building; stone or brick forming angle, corner stone, whence quoining.

Rebus – enigmatic representation of name, word, etc., by pictures, etc., suggesting its syllables.

Rector – incumbent of parish still in enjoyment of tithes.

Recusant – person who refused to attend Church of England services.

Reeve – chief magistrate of town or district.

Rood-screen – wooden or stone carved screen separating nave and choir.

Sacristy – a repository for vestments, vessels, etc., of a church.

* From a Dictionary of Geography: W. G. Moore.

See (N) – the territory under the jurisdiction of a bishop, a diocese: a city in which the authority symbolized by the throne (or a bishop, etc.) is considered to reside.

Sequestration – confiscation; appropriation.

Ship-money – impost for providing ships for navy, revival of which by Charles I was a cause of Great Rebellion.

Tenement – piece of land held by an owner; (law) any kind of permanent property, e.g. lands, rents, peerage, held of a superior; dwelling house; set of apartments used by one family.

Tenure – kind of right or title by which property is held.

Tessellated – formed of tesserae, as tessellated pavement.

Tessera (plural tesserae) – small square usually cubic block used in mosaic.

Thane – member of a rank between ordinary freemen and hereditary nobles.

Transept – transverse part of a cruciform church; either arm of this.

Vellum – fine parchment originally from skin of calf; manuscript written on this.

Verderer – judicial officer of royal forests.

Vestry – ratepayers of a parish, or representatives of these, assembled for dispatch of parochial business.

Vill – a territorial unit or division under the feudal system, consisting of a number of houses or buildings with their adjacent lands, more or less contiguous, and having a common organization.

Bibliography

NOTE
ERO – Essex Record Office
CLH – Central Library, Harlow

Alehouse Recognizance Books (ERO).
Altham Estate Map, 1616.
The Baronage of England, Dugdale.
Burke's Peerage (CLH).
The Chantry of St Petronilla, Canon J. L. Fisher.
    (Transactions of the Essex Archaeological Society).
Chapman & André Map, 1777 (CLH).
Church Histories
(a) Our Lady of Fatima.
(b) St Andrew's, Netteswell.
(c) St Mary Magdalene, Harlow Common.
The Complete Peerage, Viccary Gibbs and others.
The Deanery of Harlow, Canon J. L. Fisher.
Ecclesiastical History of Essex, Harold Smith, DD (CLH).
Encyclopaedia Britannica (CLH).
Essex Journal, Vol. 2, No. 4 (CLH).
Essex Review (various volumes) (CLH).
Florence Nightingale 1820–1910, Cecil Woodham-Smith (CLH).
The Harlow Cartulary, Transactions of the Essex Archaeological Society
    (New Series).
Harlow Guide (CLH).
Harlow New Town: a Short History of the Area which it will embrace,
    Canon J. L. Fisher (CLH).
History and Topography of the County of Essex, Wright (CLH).
History of Essex, Morant (CLH).
History of Essex, Wright (CLH).
History of Hertford, Dr F. M. Page.
The Hockerill Highway, F. H. Maud (CLH).
Kelly's Directories (Essex Record Office) (CLH, 1926 and 1937).
Leaves from a Hunting Diary in Essex, H. Beauchamp Yerburgh.
Manorial Rolls, Harlowbury Manor.
Manorial Rolls, Latton Priory and Latton Hall.
Manorial Rolls, Waltham Abbey.
National Society, Records of.
Parish of Harlow in the Nineteenth Century, D. R. Seagrave, 1965 (CLH).
Parish Registers of Latton, Netteswell, Little Parndon and Great Parndon.
Pigots Directories 1826 and 1839 (ERO).
Place-Names of Essex, Dr P. H. Reaney (CLH).
Proceedings of the Geologists' Association, Vol. 68, Part I (CLH).
Repertorium—Newcourt.
Royal Commission on Historical Monuments, England: An Inventory in
    Essex, Vol. II.
Session Rolls (ERO).
A Short History of the English Church, Gordon Crosse.

The Story of Sawbridgeworth, Book I, Sawbridgeworth WEA.
Tithe Awards & Maps.
Transactions of the Essex Archaeological Society (New Series) (CLH).
Unofficial Census of Harlow, William Boyce, 1797 (ERO).
Victoria County Histories (CLH).
White's Directories 1848 and 1863 (ERO).

Index of individuals

Index of Places

Notes

(1) Where numerous page entries relate to a place, the more significant entries appear in bold type.

(2) Map references in Roman type relate to the underlay (i.e. the historical map).

(3) Map references in Italic type relate to the overlay (i.e. the map of the new town).

Legend of historical map

☿ CHURCHES

1 – St Mary at Latton (C. of E.).
2 – St Mary and St Hugh (C. of E.).
3 – St John the Baptist. (C. of E.)
4 – St Mary the Virgin (C. of E.) Little Parndon.
5 – St Andrew (C. of E.).
7 – St Mary the Virgin (C. of E.) Great Parndon.
8 – St Mary Magdalene (C. of E.).
18 – Methodist Church.
19 – Baptist Church (Old Harlow).
20 – Baptist Church (Potter Street).
31 – St Botolph's Church.
32 – All Saints Mission Church.

☐ PUBLIC HOUSES

1 – Red Lion, Potter Street.
2 – Kings Head (D).
3 – Queens Head.
4 – Green Man.
5 – George.
6 – Marquis of Granby.
7 – Crown.
8 – Greyhound.
9 – Horn and Horseshoes.
10 – Cock.
11 – Three Horseshoes.
12 – Chequers, Commonside Road.
13 – Sun and Whalebone.
14 – Hare.
15 – Dusty Miller.
16 – Bull and Horseshoes.
17 – Chequers, Old Harlow.
18 – White Horse, Old Harlow.
19 – White Horse, Potter Street.

DB	Manors recorded in the Domesday Book.
(D)	Demolished.
	Parish boundaries.
	Geological boundaries.
▓▓▓▓	Settlements.
▒▒▒▒	Woods.